SUSTAINABLE ARCHITECTURE

Between Measurement and Meaning

Edited by

Carmela Cucuzzella
Concordia University, Canada

and

Sherif Goubran
The American University in Cairo, Egypt

Series in Built Environment

Copyright © 2021 by Cucuzzella and Goubran.

All rights reserved. No part of this publication may be reproduced, stored in a retrieval system, or transmitted in any form or by any means, electronic, mechanical, photocopying, recording, or otherwise, without the prior permission of Vernon Art and Science Inc.
www.vernonpress.com

In the Americas:
Vernon Press
1000 N West Street, Suite 1200,
Wilmington, Delaware 19801
United States

In the rest of the world:
Vernon Press
C/Sancti Espiritu 17,
Malaga, 29006
Spain

Series in Built Environment

Library of Congress Control Number: 2020942562

ISBN: 978-1-64889-207-3

Also available: 978-1-64889-047-5 [Hardback]; 978-1-64889-090-1 [PDF, E-Book]

Product and company names mentioned in this work are the trademarks of their respective owners. While every care has been taken in preparing this work, neither the authors nor Vernon Art and Science Inc. may be held responsible for any loss or damage caused or alleged to be caused directly or indirectly by the information contained in it.

Every effort has been made to trace all copyright holders, but if any have been inadvertently overlooked the publisher will be pleased to include any necessary credits in any subsequent reprint or edition.

Cover designed by Maddy Capozzi.

TABLE OF CONTENTS

LIST OF FIGURES   v

LIST OF TABLES   ix

ABOUT THE EDITORS   xi

ABOUT THE CONTRIBUTORS   xiii

ABOUT THE FOREWORD AUTHOR   xvii

FOREWORD
Walking the wire – sustainability + design in an uncertain ethos   xix

Brian R. Sinclair
University of Calgary

ACKNOWLEDGEMENTS   xxiii

INTRODUCTION
Caught between measurement and meaning   1

Carmela Cucuzzella
Concordia University

Sherif Goubran
The American University in Cairo

CHAPTER 1
Zoom-in, Zoom-out – Sustainability in the Scale(s) of Architecture   14

Anne Cormier
Université de Montréal

CHAPTER 2
Sustainable architecture as facticity, perception, and potential   24

Carmela Cucuzzella
Concordia University

CHAPTER 3
Technological trajectories: Assessing the role of sensing in design   46

Nada Tarkhan
Massachusetts Institute of Technology (MIT)

CHAPTER 4
Recognising effectiveness in sustainable design   70

Tom Jefferies
Queen's University Belfast

Laura Coucill
Manchester School of Architecture

CHAPTER 5
Connections of immaterial to sustainable tectonics   98

Izabel Amaral
Laurentian University

CHAPTER 6
Intentions and Consequences: Prototyping and Appropriate Technology   118

Ted Cavanagh
Dalhousie University

EPILOGUE   143

Carmela Cucuzzella
Concordia University

Sherif Goubran
The American University in Cairo

INDEX   147

LIST OF FIGURES

Figure 2.1	Bibliothèque du Boisé. St. Laurent, Montreal, Canada - 2014	30
Figure 2.2	The Centre for Sustainable Energy Technologies. Ningbo, China - 2008	31
Figure 2.3	Médiathèque François Villon. Bourg-la-Reine, France - 2014	33
Figure 2.4	Ningbo History Museum. Ningbo, Zhejiang, China - 2008	34
Figure 2.5	SOF - Danish National Maritime Museum. Helsingør, Denmark - 2013	35
Figure 2.6	Ballard Library. Seattle, Washington - 2013	38
Figure 2.7	Water and Life Museum complex. Hemet, California - 2008	39
Figure 3.1	Scalar analysis	47
Figure 3.2	Cycle of innovation and market adoption in the wellness field	54
Figure 3.3	Sensor kit for indoor environmental parameters	56
Figure 3.4	Preview of the online web-tool's dashboard	57
Figure 3.5	CO_2 measurements in old and new office for one working day	58
Figure 3.6	Daily circadian lighting operation	59
Figure 3.7	Lighting equivalent melanopic lux (EML) measurements for one working day	60
Figure 4.1	Visualising the complex relationship between data and space in order to demonstrate the limitations of efficiency-driven approaches to sustainable design	71
Figure 4.2	Electricity sub-station building converted into Coffee Shop, Alexandria, Sydney NSW	80
Figure 4.3	Infrastructure Space: An examination of the spatial requirements for wind and solar energy in the Scottish Highland region	82

Figure 4.4	Infrastructure Space: An examination of the spatial relationship between renewable energy production and demand in Cornwall	82
Figure 4.5	Infrastructure Space: Dispersed Urban network analysis of the Scottish Highland region in 2015/16	84
Figure 4.6	Infrastructure Space: Cornwall Garden City. Connectivity and Networks analysis of Cornwall and the Isles of Scilly	86
Figure 4.7	Winning scheme, Whitefield Housing international Housing Competition (2006). Whitefield, Nelson, UK	87
Figure 4.8	Infrastructure Space: Patterns of Power - Visualising pattern types which generate cultural landscapes; buildings augment and reveal latent contextual correlations.	88
Figure 4.9	Infrastructure Space: Patterns of Power - Geo-thermal power plant, Penzance UK	90
Figure 5.1	Tridimensional diagram summarizing Gottfried Semper's theory	102
Figure 5.2	First-year Studio assignment, study on the notions of Roofwork and Earthwork – 2018	106
Figure 5.3	The performance Dancing Geometry presented at the 3rd Nuit Blanche. Sudbury, Ontario - 2019	107
Figure 5.4	The building activities for the Ice Station. Sudbury, Ontario - 2018.	110
Figure 5.5	Ice Station's structural details. Sudbury, Ontario - 2018	111
Figure 5.6	Ice Station constructed and in its context. Sudbury, Ontario – 2018. Author's photo.	112
Figure 5.7	Details of Jean-Marc Dalpé's engraved poem on the Ice Station's horizontal boards. Sudbury, Ontario – 2018. Author's photo	113
Figure 6.1	Le Petit Cercle, Children's Theatre – 2004	119
Figure 6.2	Marché Fermier, Farmers' Market – 2014	120
Figure 6.3	Design and construction experimentation for the two featured projects	121
Figure 6.4	A map for critical clarification between prototyping and appropriate technology – focusing on the factors of the two featured projects	122

Figure 6.5	Wood cribs containing rock ballast in "Le Petit Cercle" - 2004	126
Figure 6.6	The creation of "Le Petit Cercle", showing the crib work and curvature - 2004	127
Figure 6.7	Negotiating the location of "Le Petit Cercle" on the site in reference to the existing slide - 2004	128
Figure 6.8	The 'noded-out' base connection of "Le Marché Fermier"- 2014	129
Figure 6.9	The double curvature in the plan of "Le Marché Fermier"- 2014	129
Figure 6.10	Physical model for "Le Marché Fermier"- 2014	130
Figure 6.11	Digital model for "Le Marché Fermier"- 2014	131
Figure 6.12	"Le Marché Fermier" in place - 2014	131
Figure 6.13	"Le Marché Fermier" in use - 2014	132

LIST OF TABLES

Table 2.1   General distinction between facticity, potentiality, and perception as means for sustainable architectural design inquiry   27

Table 2.2   Examples of concerns within ontological categories of facticity, potential, and perception for a sustainable architecture project   41

ABOUT THE EDITORS

Carmela Cucuzzella is the chairholder of the Concordia University Research Chair in Integrated Design, Ecology, and Sustainability for the Built Environment (IDEAS-BE). She is also an Associate Professor in the Design and Computation Arts department in the Faculty of Fine Arts, at Concordia University.

Sherif Goubran is an Instructor at the Department of Architecture at the School of Science and Engineering at the American University in Cairo (Egypt). He is also a PhD candidate in the Individualized Program at Concordia University and a Vanier Scholar (SSHRC). His interdisciplinary research is focused on sustainable building practices within the fields of design, building engineering and finance.

ABOUT THE CONTRIBUTORS

Anne Cormier

Principal at Atelier Big City, Montreal Canada
Professor, School of Architecture - Université de Montréal

Ms. Cormier is co-founder of Atelier Big City (Cormier, Cohen, Davies, architectes), a group of Montreal architects recognized for the quality of its architectural and urban projects. Founded in 1987, Atelier Big City received the Prix de Rome in Architecture from the Canada Council for the Arts, the Governor General's medal and the grand prize in architecture from the Ordre des architectes du Québec. The group has presented and shown their work in Quebec, Canada and abroad and has been invited to teach at Cornell University, Rensselaer Polytechnic Institute, University of Toronto and University of Calgary. Anne Cormier is also a Professor at the School of Architecture at Université de Montréal, where she has served as director from 2007 to 2015. She is affiliated with the Laboratoire d'étude de l'architecture potentielle (LEAP), an inter-university group dedicated to research on the design process in architecture. She is a member of the National Capital Commission's Advisory Committee on Planning, Design and Realty in Ottawa. She regularly sits on other committees dedicated to excellence in architectural and urban projects and on architectural juries.

Carmela Cucuzzella

Associate Professor, Design and Computation Arts, Faculty of Fine Arts, Concordia University
Concordia University Research Chair in Integrated Design, Ecology, And Sustainability for the Built Environment (www.ideas-be.ca)

Carmela Cucuzzella is an Associate Professor in the Design and Computation Arts department and is a holder of the Concordia University Research Chair in Integrated Design, Ecology and Sustainability for the Built Environment (www.ideas-be.ca). Her research work is framed within the broad domain of design studies where she investigates questions of sustainable design for urban living. Her varied background and expertise in environmental and social life cycle analysis, in green building rating systems, and in design and architecture, allow her to adopt a framework revolving around design's interrelated dimensions of the cognitive-instrumental, the moral-practical and the aesthetic-expressive forms of conception and discourse with a focus on the sustainable city.

Izabel Amaral

Assistant Professor, McEwen School of Architecture. Laurentian University Sudbury

Izabel Amaral teaches architecture and structural design at the McEwen School of Architecture where she is an Assistant Professor. A Canadian citizen holding a doctorate from the Université de Montréal, this Brazilian architect has been living in Canada since 2005. Her research focus is on the theories and histories of architecture, where she investigates the design process of architecture, as well as the relationship between technique, construction and aesthetics according to locally skilled and cultural approaches. Her teaching practice involves collaborative design processes, hands-on learning and critical thinking. She has gained significant professional experience of more than five years in agency practice, including three years as a partner, and five years of teaching in Northeastern Brazil, Quebec, and Ontario.

Laura Coucill

Senior Lecturer Manchester School of Architecture

Laura is an award-winning designer with experience in residential and commercial architectural practice. She has held teaching and research positions at Schools of Architecture in Manchester Sheffield and Birmingham. Her research is principally concerned with the implications of policy for architectural design. Her design research methodology foregrounds data-mapping; a method which unites design skill and geolocation to engage with the dynamic, cross-thematic and multifaceted nature of space, which is developed through historic and contemporary urban theory to provide insights into lived experience and resilience. Past work has enabled local planning and policy decision making in Stockport (UK) regional cross-cutting analysis in the Scottish Highlands and Cornwall (UK).

Nada Tarkhan

PhD Candidate, MIT
(previously, Sustainability Consultant, ARUP and Adjunct Professor, Northeastern University)

Nada is a sustainability consultant with extensive industry experience. She has worked in multiple fields of practice including Sustainability and Building Physics Consulting at Arup and Project Management at Jones Lang LaSalle. Nada received her master's degree from the Harvard Graduate School of Design and is currently a PhD candidate at MIT. Her work focuses on enhancing occupied environments through careful assessments of ventilation, daylighting and material use. In addition to this, Nada has been an Adjunct Professor at Northeastern University, where she has lectured on Bio-climatic strategies and energy accounting in design.

Ted Cavanagh

Professor, School of Architecture and Director of Coastal Studio - Dalhousie University

Dr. Cavanagh's research focuses on the design and construction of innovative building prototypes appropriate to the coastal communities of Nova Scotia. He studies the history of innovation in construction technology and its influence on building design. He is the founder of the design/build exchange for North American and European schools of architecture.

Tom Jefferies

Professor of Future Cities, the School of Natural and Built Environment - Queen's University Belfast

Tom Jefferies is Professor of Future Cities in the School of Natural and Built Environment, a prize-winning architect and urban designer. Prior to joining Queen's University Belfast, he was Head of the Manchester School of Architecture (2011-19), and Birmingham School of Architecture. He has taught, lectured and examined internationally. Tom's research investigates relationships between culture, space, landscape process to propose new forms of contemporary urbanism. Expertise in architecture, urban design, landscape, master planning and design codes, architectural history, theory and context, sustainability and heritage as a basis for developing symbiotic relationships between research and inter-disciplinary practice.

Sherif Goubran

Instructor, Department of Architecture, School of Science and Engineering. The American University in Cairo (AUC-Egypt)
PhD candidate, Individualized Program. Concordia University

Sherif is an instructor at the Department of Architecture at the School of Science and Engineering at the American University in Cairo (Egypt). He is also a PhD candidate in the Individualized Program (INDI) at Concordia University, a Vanier Scholar (SSHRC) and a Concordia Public Scholars program alumnus (2019-2020). He is conducting interdisciplinary research on building sustainability assessment within the fields of design, building engineering and real-estate finance. His PhD research investigates the alignment between sustainable design practices and global sustainable development goals. Sherif completed a MASc in building engineering and a BSc in architecture. Sherif is actively engaged in several research laboratories, centers, and groups.

ABOUT THE FOREWORD AUTHOR

Brian R. Sinclair

Professor of Architecture + Environmental Design & Former Dean, School of Architecture, Planning + Landscape, University of Calgary
President, sinclairstudio inc., Calgary Canada

Dr. Brian R. Sinclair, PhD DrHC FRAIC AIA (Intl) is Professor of Architecture + Environmental Design, and former Dean, in the University of Calgary's School of Architecture, Planning + Landscape. Brian is president of sinclairstudio inc., a multi-disciplinary design|research corporation engaged in an array of global projects. He holds postgraduate degrees in architecture and psychology. An educator and practitioner, Sinclair`s expertise and explorations span from science to art. Professional memberships include the American Institute of Architects, Union of Mongolian Architects, Society of Nepalese Architects, Council for Tall Buildings + Urban Habitat, and Fellowship in the Royal Architectural Institute of Canada. His doctoral degree (University of Missouri) focused on an innovative holistic design + planning framework to improve the quality of life for some of the world's poorest people. Scholarship includes professional practice, design methods, open building, agile architecture, strategic planning, integrated design, environmental psychology, international development, systems & sustainability, and the collision of science + spirit.

FOREWORD
Walking the wire – sustainability + design in an uncertain ethos

Brian R. Sinclair
University of Calgary

"Smile
You don't have to spend your days in clouds
Hiding from the sun
Take a look around and see
It's not that easy for anyone"

Chris Rea, 1988.

Today we live in uncertain, unprecedented and unpredictable times. The world we knew – one characterized by reasonable levels of stability and a modicum of sureness – is now dramatically dissolving and disconcertingly dissipating, only to be replaced with a milieu all too commonly cast as chaotic, intense, polarized and improbable. For architects and environmental designers, recent times have proven particularly difficult, in part due to a longstanding subscription to the static, iconic and permanent, and in part due to an ever-increasing marginalization of the services they deliver to societies in flux. That said, the turbulence that has arrived so abruptly into our cities, communities and lives now offers opportunities for positive change through the vehicle of design and via our toolsets, our mindsets, our means and our methods. While architecture in a bricks and mortar age celebrated solidity and hardness, environmental design today finds itself in a place where agility, softness, responsivity and responsibility loom large.

Sustainability factors centrally into such musings. With decreasing resources, escalating climate change, growing tension and heightened risk, architecture finds itself in an interesting position. Undeniably part of the problem of environmental decay, buildings contribute in serious ways to our planet's demise. However, in light of rising greenhouse gas emissions, burgeoning landfill contributions, declining public health and other distressing developments, architecture and environmental design proffers hope. Design by its nature is well equipped to tackle highly complex challenges and penetratingly perplexing problems. Architects, landscape architects, interior, industrial and urban designers, to name but a few vital players, all hold strategic keys to move us in the right directions. That said, many strategic adjustments and tactical maneuvers are required, including in realms political, to unleash the power of design within and to a world in need.

Carmela Cucuzzella and Sherif Goubran's new book, entitled "Sustainable Architecture – Between Measurement and Meaning" arrives at a significant point in time. Their edited volume challenges many of the assumptions that have developed in recent years concerning the concept of 'sustainability'. Sustainability is a term that has amplified in reach and expanded in meaning, being widely embraced by many sectors of society in an effort to turn a ship that is perceptibly careening towards disaster. However, with such a strong uptake comes confusion and, at times disarray. In many ways and in many corners we encounter jargon fatigue, sensing on one hand the imperative to act yet often unclear concerning which steps to take. One major obstacle to moving ahead with purpose and success is the West's obsession with metrics, facts and truths. Metrics can miss their mark. Facts can shift based on the efficacy of our instrumentation and the potency of our theories. Truths are regularly relative. An all too common mantra espoused by a wealth of players suggests, "If you can't count it, it doesn't count". However, not all that matters, or that might or should reckon in our equations, can be readily counted or easily characterized.

The new edited volume takes a crucial step forward in its direct challenge of conventional thinking on sustainability. Highlighting the proposition that sustainability must be cast beyond math and measurement, the various chapters serve to open our minds to new ways of seeing, thinking and acting. Beyond the easily quantified dimensions of an environmental design project, whether energy consumption, water usage or volatile organic compounds levels, resides aspects that inject substance and meaning into our journeys. The various invited authors, across their diverse and thoughtful chapters, reveal features of architecture and design that, at the end of the day, prove the most essential to a more sustainable world. Rather than merely discounting the value of evidence, research and matters empirical, the authors accept the power of contemporary science while moving beyond to capture more ethereal dimensions of inhabitation that are vital to realizing truly sustainable cities, neighborhoods, buildings, places and spaces.

Modern civilization has, on numerous counts, slipped into a milieu where dualistic thinking has obscured our ability to see with clarity and definition. We cast situations as polarities: art-science, poetic-pragmatic, soft-hard, intuitive-rational, analog-digital, heart-head, feeling-thinking, and so on. This clinical parsing of our world, and the accompanying pressures to then take sides, has been destructive and counter-productive. It has ushered in spheres of fragmentation, isolation, separation, disconnection and disenfranchisement. Further, and all too often, one side of the spectrum has been advantaged above the other, rendering science, technology, engineering and math above other means of understanding. Considering my own world & self views, informed by my posturing as an architect and psychologist and influenced by my background spanning science and art, I see the present situation as dire and in need of numerous and concerted surgical strikes. At the center of the challenge is the need for balance, equilibrium and holism. In my holistic framework for design and planning, I underscore the need for harmonious interplay of agility, fitness, diversity and delight. This last quality, one that acknowledges beauty, pursues happiness and accepts things incomprehensible, has been controversial – in large part due to its inability to be empirically defined. That said, the notion of delight carries as much cache and worth as any components of a project that can be quickly counted, simply metered or methodically measured.

The present edited book is significant in many ways, but perhaps most vividly through its inclusion of an array of facets that make our sojourns interesting, satisfying and meaningful. Sustainability is far more than operational savings, water conservation and reduced embodied energy. Sustainability must be deeper and richer, accounting for more indeterminate and qualitative features such as social value, aesthetic wealth, amplified well-being, cultural vibrancy, and spiritual tilling. Cucuzzella and Goubran's timely volume serves to apply the brakes to our amplified techno-centric trajectory, affording the reader an opportunity to consider the richness of design and its capacity to provide more appropriate, more sensitive and more human environments for living, playing, working, surviving and thriving.

While the environmental design professions have made serious strides forward in the last several decades, with respect to reducing ecological footprints and increasing quality of life, much more work stands ahead. While initial building rating approaches were overly simplistic and too narrow, recent iterations and advancements have moved the needle towards individual health and societal well-being. Such progress is encouraging and essential. However given recent crises, including the arrival of a global pandemic, the rise of anti-racist movements, the growing political tensions apparent within and between nations, the growing wealth divide, to name but a few daunting challenges in our lives, there is an urgency for architects and allied professionals to act. Such action must consider the behavior of complex systems – we cannot continue with piecemeal gestures and partial steps that too often are uncoordinated, inappropriate and impotent. To my mind r/evolution will demand a far-reaching embrace that encircles science, the arts, the humanities, culture, context and spirituality. We must not be fearful on treading on ground unexplored and anticipating collisions unprecedented. We must also be willing to invest the time and resources required to tailor solutions to place and circumstance – in a new domain of sustainability one size does not fit all and universal answers are unlikely. Fortunately, science and technology, wisely and humbly coupled with common sense and human-centric orientation, can generate place-based solutions that meet expectations, extend comfort and reduce impact. An era of smart cities, intelligent buildings and responsive spaces is possible, and should be efficacious if driven by both artificial intelligence and mortal compassion. As we confront unfathomable uncertainty we must learn to take greater risks, to accept that not everything is comprehensible and to grasp that steadiness, moderation and open-mindedness are central aspirations.

The arrival of *Sustainable Architecture – Between Measurement and Meaning* is a welcomed addition to our national and international conversations on the future of cities and societies. Through its varied and compelling chapters, the book calls for a reconsideration of design in light of rapidly shifting realities in our new millennium. The authors provide us with differing, thought-provoking yet complementary vantage points for evaluating our place, processes and progress as we dwell on an ever more distressed planet. Carmela Cucuzzella and Sherif Goubran are commended for their vision, efforts and success in confronting the status quo, and for shepherding a talented ensemble of authors to join them on this acute journey.

Dr. Brian R. Sinclair, PhD DrHC FRAIC AIA (Intl)

ACKNOWLEDGEMENTS

We acknowledge the financial support provided through the Concordia University Research Chair program and the Social Sciences and Humanities Research Council of Canada, without which this project could not have taken form. We would like thank Maddy Capozzi for developing the design of the book cover. In addition, we greatly appreciate the excellent copy-editing and editorial assistance we received from Ian Anthony Taylor. We would like to thank Professor Terrance Galvin for his careful review of the manuscript. We would also like to thank Professor Brian Sinclair for his insightful foreword, which captures the essence of the collection. Finally, we feel greatly indebted to all the contributors to this collection for their flexibility and patience throughout the development of the project.

INTRODUCTION
Caught between measurement and meaning

Carmela Cucuzzella

Concordia University

Sherif Goubran

The American University in Cairo

INTRODUCTION

We often think about sustainable architecture as a way of designing and constructing buildings to exist in harmony with the environment around them. We think in terms of reducing negative impacts on flora, fauna, natural resources, our communities, and our economy. For many of these imperative objectives, measurement is key to designing sustainably. But how do sustainable buildings affect the interrelated qualities of our built environment, though, and how do they relate more generally to quality of life for all living species?

Philippe Boudon has stated that "measure[ment] in architectural design necessarily associates some qualitative and quantitative, but it is understandable that this follows the notion that it is not possible to have any measurement without meaning" (Boudon 1999a, p.9, translated by authors). If we agree that measurement consists of assigning a number to a characteristic of an object or event so that it can be compared with other objects or events, then the process inherently embeds the relevance of the qualities of its object or event. The practice of sustainable architecture involves an interminable list of measurements meant to enumerate environmental damages and optimizations of processes. These quantitative facts and figures proceed only because there is an intention to envision, understand and manage the harmful impacts of architecture and construction. Sustainable architecture has been overrun by measurements, but at what devastating architectural cost, and more importantly, to what concrete sustainable development outcomes?

Despite all that we know about the sustainability crisis today, despite the many sustainability parameters we measure or manage, and despite our adeptness at developing new eco-technologies, the rate of environmental damages is still increasing across the planet (Venter et al., 2016). While population growth is one of the most well-known factors affecting the environment (Ehrlich, 1968), it alone does not explain this phenomenon. All sectors of development contribute a share of this destruction: i.e. transportation, food, building, and infrastructure, etc. But the prominent effects of buildings on the environment have been long established. On a global scale, buildings (during construction and operations) consume approximately 40% of the energy supply, 30% of the raw materials, 12% of the global freshwater, and to globally generate up to 20% of the global GHG, 40% of the total landfill waste, and 20% of the water effluents.

Indeed, energy and emissions reduction goals are not new; they were first propagated during the 1973 oil crisis (Peffer et al., 2011) and have been deeply embedded in the technical advancement of buildings since. In many cases, it is technology that is driving innovation in the built environment (De Dear, 2011). Similarly, the technological emphasis of resource efficiency for addressing environmental degradation systematically developed throughout the 1980s and 1990s began to reach its limitations around the turn of the century (Cucuzzella, 2009; Rossi, 2004; Papanek, 2000). In more recent years, energy infrastructure and grid limitation have pushed researchers to explore means of controlling energy demand – especially during peak hours (Zehir et al., 2019). When the strategy of eco-efficiency is adopted at the exclusion of other design approaches, it tends to subordinate central complex concerns of design to a stated mission (Rotor, 2014; Guy & Moore, 2005; Hansen & Knudstrup, 2005).

The strategy underlying eco-efficiency has as its goal the *prevention* of risks – the reduction of risks that are known and measurable. Such a goal is the product of a society where there is little tolerance for the occurrence of risks and significant effort put towards mitigating their outcomes (Cucuzzella, 2016a). Given the dual crises of climate change and environmental degradation, this is quite justified. However, research has shown that overuse of eco-efficiencies on their own may actually lead to increased environmental impacts. At times, this may be related to unintended outcomes of performance optimizations, and at other times, to unrelated secondary or tertiary activities or sectors (Alcott, 2008; Herring & Roy, 2007; Sorrell, 2007; Madlener & Alcott, 2006). Over 150 years ago, William Stanley Jevons discovered that gains in energy efficiency ultimately lead to greater energy consumption (Polimeni, Mayumi, Giampietro, & Alcott, 2008), and his paradox shows up in various aspects of life even today[1]. The phenomenon is clearly apparent in residential energy consumption.

---

[1] For example, the wider that designers build a given highway, the less traffic jams are

For an example of this, we will look to Canada. The Standing Senate Committee on Energy, the Environment and Natural Recourses indicated in their November 2018 report that, despite the substantial efficiency gains achieved since the early 2000s, the building sector's overall GHG emissions have only decreased by 3 percent. Furthermore, the building sector's overall energy consumption is increasing and is expected to continue doing so for several more years. (The Senate Standing Committee - Energy the Environment and Natural Resources, 2018). In fact, since the 1990s, energy efficiency in the residential sector has improved by 45 percent[2], but the sector's overall energy consumption has increased by almost 7 percent[3]. Meanwhile, the country's population has increased by only 21 percent[4].

What this indicates is that, while new technologies and improved performance measures offer resource efficiency and economic gains (Berardi, 2012), they alone cannot be the answer to the problems of unsustainability that humanity faces (Jackson, 2004).

Even knowing all of this, though, environmental management approaches, exemplified by certifications, assessment tools and standards, are most often associated with achieving sustainability in the built environment[5]. And while they played a vital role in popularizing "green" buildings, their normalized and fragmented design approaches show some major weaknesses (Díaz-López et al., 2019; Cucuzzella, 2019; Riascos et al., 2015). Additionally, the slow and accumulative nature of codes and standards might not be capable of coping efficiently with the complexity of the challenges we are facing (Goubran, Masson, et al., 2020). These inescapable means of standardized evaluation for sustainable architecture are not questioned here. Rather, it is the strict reliance on the focus of measurable eco-efficiencies alone that is challenged in this collection (Cucuzzella, 2016b, 2009). What we focus on, in particular, is when this behaviour leads to the production of more and more strictly-defined 'greener' buildings and infrastructures and doesn't consider a broader context – spatially, temporally, socially, culturally, or otherwise. In reality, building *sustainably* requires dedicating equal attention to a structure's environmental, social, cultural and economic

---

expected. However, the opposite occurs. The wider the highway, the more traffic congestion is experienced (Duranton & Turner, 2011).

[2] This is measured by calculating the energy consumption per square metre in the residential building sector.

[3] http://oee.rncan.gc.ca/publications/statistics/trends11/chapter3.cfm

[4] To catch up with a rapidly growing population, we are now constructing more buildings at faster rates.

[5] Mainly because because of their ability to assess specific eco-efficiencies, performance optimizations or improvements in buildings and infrastructures.

impacts. This means moving the design and development focus beyond the measurement and reduction of damages and towards the aim of protecting the environment, promoting cultural development, encouraging local economic development, and addressing social challenges in our communities. In this way, sustainable buildings can go beyond the materials and energy they use to proactively contribute to society (Goubran, 2019a). These inter- and intra-building interactions can and should happen at a variety of scales.

Let us consider a short thought experiment on how considering scale can have a number of positive impacts on sustainable architecture. During the process of design, the architect necessarily articulates numerous types of scale. For example, they assess the scalar considerations of environmental technologies or how the scale of the building, the neighbourhood, or the region can contribute to an overall reduction in energy use. Scale can even be considered in terms of the economic gauge in which the occupiable space will be monetarily calculated. The functional scale deals with the comparisons and distribution of floor space. The structural scale is used to measure how spaces are best supported in ways that won't infringe on spatial qualities. Even the scale of the model becomes a means for deliberation to help better understand specific constructive optimizations. Indeed, with today's prevalent digitalization of architecture models, the digital model is also a key mechanism for the measurement of various environmental characteristics (Picon, 2010). In addition to questions directly related to a building's design, scale must also refer to the physical and social elements that surround the structure. This means the relationship of the new building with the street, the adjacent buildings, the in-between green spaces, and the neighbourhood. The conception of architectural scale must also consider the project's relationship with the community, the cultures within the community, the diversity of the individuals, etc. When ensuring the complexity of such scalar elements - varying models, spatial comparisons, or neighbouring considerations - none can be ignored. Conceiving of sustainable architecture through the lens of scale necessarily encompasses both measurement and meaning. Philippe Boudon, as early as 1999, unfolded the notion of scale into various constituent operations (Boudon, 2002, 1999a, 1999b). According to him, the term 'scale' in architecture can refer to three levels: (1) the aesthetic quality (grandness), (2) the quantitative elements (measurements), and (3) its meaningfulness as intellectually conceived (relevance).

Given this experiment, it is clear that dependence on environmental management methods and tools alone for achieving sustainability in buildings has to be challenged. On their own, reductive, technologically-focused approaches have led to counterproductive outcomes, of which we can identify three:

First, both environment management tools and eco-technologies were developed based on their ability to forecast or mitigate *predictable* risks in the climate and sustainability crises. This is, in one sense, a strength, as it allows architects to lessen potentially dangerous outcomes of a buildable design. It is also, however, a weakness, since people that inhabit these superbly optimized buildings do not always comply with design expectations. The diversity and unpredictability of human behaviours is a given, yet is not typically considered in the environmental accounting of building design, nor the future evolution of a space and its functions (Khasreen, Banfill, & Menzies, 2009)[6]. This has resulted in significant divergences between actual and promised or predicted performance in sustainable buildings (Amiri et al., 2019; Newsham et al., 2009; Stoppel & Leite, 2013; Yudelson & Meyer, 2013).

Second, the narrow focus of most environmental management tools tends to fragment a given design problem into a finite set of variables that rarely captures the complexity of a given context and design situation (physically, socially, or culturally), resulting in its being given very little thought, or even none at all (Farmer, 1996; Guy & Farmer, 2000; Rossi, 2004). This fragmented analysis of whole projects in terms of their many individual parts is problematic, especially when thinking about capturing synergies and project coherence. At times, it even results in counter-productive solutions[7]. This is a generalization of the above thought experiment on the question of scale. Simply thinking about scale when designing sustainable architecture would already break the current normative framework of environmental management tools. This is but one example. Herein lies the epitome of tension between measurement and meaning.

Third, the prescriptive or normative nature of sustainable evaluation tools leaves little room for exploring profoundly innovative solutions (Cucuzzella, 2019; Goubran, 2019b). In many cases, the intuitive and visionary manner in which certain architects design their projects is at odds with the predictability and measurability needed for the optimally efficient design of specific eco-features. Recent designs of buildings and infrastructures have shown that prevalent sustainable approaches remain rather normative when experimental solutions are avoided as too economically risky (Cucuzzella, 2019; Ravetz, 2004; Stirling, 2006). It can even be suggested that normative and empirical sustainable design methods marginalize certain design approaches (Goubran, 2019b). This becomes problematic when entire designs are focused on performance instead of a

---

[6] Indeed, unpredictability is perceived as a special case where decision processes require alternative methods (Haag & Kaupenjohann, 2001).

[7] Putting into consideration that the profound problems facing humanity cannot be solved through technology alone, since it is unable to address questions of social or cultural conditions, in particular collective awareness and individual responsibilities

project's aesthetic-experiential qualities (Cucuzzella, 2016b) This limits the ability of designers to reflect and adapt to local and regional realities, to discover new design solutions, or to achieve quality and leadership in design through reflective practices (Nelson & Stolterman, 2012; Schön, 1983).

OVERVIEW OF COLLECTION

Why has sustainable architecture continued to focus primarily on techno-sciences and managerial methods rather than more all-encompassing, qualitative approaches to designing places for dwelling?

Given that the evolution of the architectural discipline and profession is necessarily shifting beyond its historic foundations as the global demand for living and working spaces continues to grow exponentially, how is this convergence between measurement and meaning occurring? While the field of architecture is bounded by its history, its potency of meanings and symbolic capital, the field of sustainability is unbounded and straddles multiple professions and disciplines (Owen & Dovey, 2008). Sustainability has been based on objective science and has perpetuated a mechanistic worldview, yet it is this very mechanistic worldview that has allowed us to identify current pressing environmental and social conditions. So, there is a reluctance to abandon such scientific knowledge when designing buildings for the future. Architects that engage with sustainable practices must aim to reconcile both fields. Yet, architects and designers are already realizing that sustainability is quickly moving towards a technocratic paradigm (Steele, 2005; Vandevyvere & Heynen, 2014). This may be one of the reasons why the field of sustainable architecture is often at odds with the field of architecture.

Yet, the majority of research on sustainable architecture today emphasises the quantitative dimension and is occasionally received by scholarly critiques pointing to its lack of socio-cultural meanings. Every day, tens, if not hundreds, of new articles, books and reports present methods, technologies, and standards for achieving sustainability in architecture and the built environment. Of course, technology will continue to have a place in all aspects of society and humanity, and its importance is not doubted. But as new materials, technological gadgets, and data are increasingly being considered as the staples of the future of architecture, we are losing sight of the core concerns of expression, contextuality, functionality and aesthetics, which have long been the historical foundation of architecture as a profession and discipline. As we increasingly embrace technology, we may be pushing architecture into a managerial science. This demonstrates Panayiota Pyla's view that "sustainability is constantly running the danger of turning into a totalizing doctrine that subsumes critical thinking" (2008). As we move towards a technocratic sustainable future, we lose the humanity of architecture – the reciprocal relationship between humans creating meaningful spaces that in turn condition the future of humanity. What the literature lacks is a critical inquiry on the meaning of sustainable architecture and alternative ways forward– those beyond reactionary responses to the techno-centric modus operandi.

In a time of competing solutions, this book steps back to reflect on why our actions are still not slowing down global social and environmental degradation. It acknowledges that architecture will continue to occupy a vital role in our world; it is the field that creates our places of dwelling, of business, of production, of leisure, of learning, and of creation. It also acknowledges that buildings are deeply connected to the historic contexts of their sites and play a key role in defining our social relations and our connection to the spaces we occupy and use. Beyond the abstract measurement and accounting that occupies the epicentre of the green buildings sector today, this book aims to re-examine sustainable architecture and the intricate frictions between measurement and meanings that can lead to *sustainability*.

Through a short collection of critical essays prepared by scholars and practitioners, the book exposes that sustainability in architecture is a human and social science that lies at the intersection of measurements and meanings. It reveals that sustainable architecture can still operate in a dialectic space of expression rather than as a manifesto for either the technical or socio-cultural extremes. That architecture is still the profession of meaning-making – far beyond a simple holder of activities and eco-technologies. That the human – intuition, senses, and skills – still holds the key to unravelling alternative futures of sustainable built spaces. And that most importantly, humans still have a place in sustainable architecture.

This book seeks to move beyond the ever-increasing development of eco-technologies and their measured eco-efficiencies towards the investigation of sustainability in a broader, more interdisciplinary manner. It provides a cross-sectional investigation that communicates different sustainability approaches, theories, and practices. The collection is made of six contributions, complemented by prefaces for each chapter (prepared by the co-editors). The contributions were selected based on their ability to bridge theory and practice and to specifically uncover the often-unexplored tension between meanings and measurements of sustainable architecture. In the **first chapter**, Anne Cormier tackles the question of measurement in architecture, in all its diverse forms, to highlight that the human has no place in an architecture of infinite scales. In the **second chapter**, Carmela Cucuzzella explores sustainable architecture's different modes of *being*, basing her exploration on the work of Jean-Paul Sartre. The theoretical exploration exposes the inadequacy of sustainable architecture design being simply an exercise of facts (facticity) or as an expressive means of communicating 'greenness' (perception) for meeting long-term sustainability expectations. In the **third chapter**, Nada Tarkhan investigates how sustainable architecture discourse and rhetoric are influenced by technological developments and market demand. Nada exposes a vicious cycle where the qualitative dimensions of the architecture are marginalized. Tom Jefferies and Laura Coucil further explore the notion of data representation in sustainable architecture in **chapter four**. They propose that re-placing the human and physical dimension in sustainable architecture can help drive the focus away from efficiency-driven metrics towards design for effectiveness. Chapters five and six reintegrate sustainable architecture in practice. In **chapter five**, Izabel Amaral employs the theory of tectonics to further explore the unquantifiable and immaterial dimensions of sustainable architecture. She proposes that the process of making – or architecture as a craft – can act as the mediating force between the meaning and measurement in sustainable design. Finally, in **chapter six**, Ted Cavanagh further investigates the dimensions of *making* sustainable architecture: the global vs. local, and tailored vs. replicable. Through a mixed theoretical and practice-based investigation, he highlights that the confounding of these scales can remove the local character that should necessarily define sustainable building design. The book then concludes with a short epilogue that aims to create a space for readers to critically reflect on and interact with the concepts presented.

REFERENCES

Alcott, B. (2008, April). Ipat and Rebound Effect. Paper presented at *Economic Degrowth for Ecological Sustainability and Social Equity*. Paris, France.

Amiri, A., Ottelin, J., & Sorvari, J. (2019). Are LEED-certified buildings energy-efficient in practice? *Sustainability (Switzerland), 11*(6). https://doi.org/10.3390/su11061672

Boudon, P. (1999a). «Échelle» En Architecture Et Au-De Là Mesurer L'espace; Dépasser Le Modèle Géométrique. *Les annales de la recherche urbain, 0180-930-III*(82), 5-13.

Boudon, P. (1999b). Semiotics and Architecture: The Notion of Scale and Charles S. Peirce's Categories. *Nordisk Arkitekturforskning, 1*, 19-25.

Boudon, P. (2002). Echelle(S) - L'architecturologie Comme Travail D'épistémologue La Bibliotheque. Economica.

Cucuzzella, C. (2009). The limits of current evaluation methods in a context of sustainable design: prudence as a new framework. *International Journal of Design Engineering, 2*(3), 243–261. https://doi.org/10.1504/IJDE.2009.030174

Cucuzzella, C. (2016a). Creativity, sustainable design and risk management. *Journal of Cleaner Production, 135*, 1548–1558. https://doi.org/10.1016/j.jclepro.2015.12.076

Cucuzzella, C. (2016b). Tensions between Expert Evaluations and Qualitative Judgment in Canadian Architectural Competitions. In J. E. Anderson, G. B. Zettersten, & M. Rönn (Eds.), *Architectural Competitions as Institution and Process* (pp. 117–138). The Royal Institute of Technology.

Cucuzzella, C. (2019). The normative turn in environmental architecture. *Journal of Cleaner Production, 219*, 552–565. https://doi.org/10.1016/j.jclepro.2019.02.084

De Dear, R. (2011). Revisiting an old hypothesis of human thermal perception: Alliesthesia. *Building Research and Information, 39*(2), 108–117. https://doi.org/10.1080/09613218.2011.552269

Díaz-López, C., Carpio, M., Martín-Morales, M., & Zamorano, M. (2019). Analysis of the scientific evolution of sustainable building assessment methods. *Sustainable Cities and Society, 49*(February), 101610. https://doi.org/10.1016/j.scs.2019.101610

Duranton, G., & Tuner, M. A. (2011). The Fundamental Law of Road Congestion: Evidence from Us Cities. *American Economic Review 101* (October), 2616–2652.

Ehrlich, P. R. (1968). *The Population Bomb*. Buccaneer Books.

Farmer, J., (1996). *Green Shift: Towards a Green Sensibility in Architecture*. Butterworth Architecture in association with WWF-UK.

Goubran, S. (2019a, June 10). Opinion: Let's build sustainably, not just "green". *Montreal Gazette*, 1–4. https://montrealgazette.com/opinion/opinion-lets-build-sustainably-not-just-green

Goubran, S. (2019b). Sustainability in architectural design projects – a semiotic understanding. *Social Semiotics*. https://doi.org/10.1080/10350330.2019.1681062

Goubran, S., Masson, T., & Walker, T. (2020). Diagnosing the local suitability of high-rise timber construction. *Building Research & Information, 48*(1), 101–123. https://doi.org/10.1080/09613218.2019.1631700

Guy, S., & Farmer, G. (2000). Contested Constructions: The competing logics of green buildings and ethics. In W. Fox (Ed.), *Ethics and The Built Environment* (pp. 73–87). Routledge.

Guy, S. & Moore, S. A. (2005). Reflection and Engagement: Towards Pluralist Practices of Sustainable Architecture. In S. Guy & S. Moore (Eds.) *Sustainable Architectures: Cultures and Natures in Europe and North America*. Spon Press.

Haag, D., & Kaupenjohann, M. (2001). Parameters, prediction, post-normal science and the precautionary principle—a roadmap for modelling for decision-making. *Ecological Modelling, 144*(1), 45–60. https://doi.org/10.1016/S0304-3800(01)00361-1

Hansen, H. T. R., & Knudstrup, M.A. (2005). The Integrated Design Process (IDP): a more holistic approach to sustainable architecture. *The 2005 World Sustainable Building Conference*, 894–901.

Herring, H., & Roy, R. (2007). Technological Innovation, Energy Efficient Design and the Rebound Effect. *Technovation 27*(4), 194-203.

Jackson, T. (2004). Negotiating Sustainable Consumption: A Review of the Consumption Debate and its Policy Implications. *Energy & Environment, 15*(6), 1027–1051. https://doi.org/10.1260/0958305043026573

Khasreen, M., Banfill, P. F., & Menzies, G. (2009). Life-Cycle Assessment and the Environmental Impact of Buildings: A Review. *Sustainability, 1*(3), 674–701. https://doi.org/10.3390/su1030674

Madlener, R., & Alcott, B. (2006). Energy Rebound and Economic Growth: A Review of the Main Issues and Research Needs. In *Proceedings of the 5th International Biennial Workshop "Advances in Energy Studies – Perspectives into Energy Future"*. Porto Venere, Italy.

Nelson, H. G., & Stolterman, E. (2012). *The Design Way: Intentional Change in an Unpredictable World* (2nd ed.). The MIT Press.

Newsham, G. R., Mancini, S., & Birt, B. J. (2009). Do LEED-certified buildings save energy? Yes, but.... *Energy and Buildings*, *41*(8), 897–905. https://doi.org/10.1016/j.enbuild.2009.03.014

Owen, C., & Dovey, K.(2008). Fields of Sustainable Architecture. *The Journal of Architecture, 13*(1), 9-21.

Peffer, T., Pritoni, M., Meier, A., Aragon, C., & Perry, D. (2011). How people use thermostats in homes: A review. *Building and Environment, 46*(12), 2529–2541. https://doi.org/10.1016/j.buildenv.2011.06.002

Picon, A.(2010). *Digital Culture in Architecture: An Introduction for the Design Professions* (1st ed.) Birkhäuser.

Polimeni, J. M., Mayumi, K., Giampietro M., & Alcott, B. (2008). *The Jevons Paradox and the Myth of Resource Efficiency Improvements*. Earthscan Publications,.

Pyla, P. (2008, April). Counter-Histories of Sustainability. *Archis*, 1–13. volumeproject.org/counter-histories-of-sustainability/

Ravetz, J. (2004). The Post-Normal Science of Precaution. *Futures 36*(3), 347-357.

Riascos, C. E. M., Romero, J. F. A., & Riascos, L. A. M. (2015). Classification of Assessment Methods for Analyzing Sustainability in Buildings. *Journal of Civil Engineering and Architecture Research, 2*(10), 976–984.

Rossi, M. (2004). Reaching the Limits of Quantitative Life Cycle Assessment. In *Clean Production Action*. European Commission.

Rotor (2014). *Behind the Green Door: A Critical Look at Sustainable Architecture through 600 Objects*. Oslo Architecture Triennale.

Schön, A. D. (1983). *The Reflective Practitioner*. Basic Books.

Steele, J. (2005). *Ecological architecture : a critical history 1900-today*. Thames & Hudson.

Stirling, A. (2006). Precaution, Foresight and Sustainability: Reflection and Reflexivity in the Governance of Science and Technology. In *Reflexive Governance for Sustainable Development*. Edward Elgar Publishing. https://doi.org/10.4337/9781847200266.00020

Stoppel, C. M., & Leite, F. (2013). Evaluating building energy model performance of LEED buildings: Identifying potential sources of error through aggregate analysis. *Energy and Buildings, 65*, 185–196. https://doi.org/10.1016/j.enbuild.2013.04.016

The Senate Standing Committee - Energy the Environment and Natural Resources. (2018). *Reducing Greenhouse Gas Emissions from Canada's Built Environment*.

Vandevyvere, H., & Heynen, H. (2014). Sustainable Development, Architecture and Modernism: Aspects of an Ongoing Controversy. *Arts, 3*(4), 350–366. https://doi.org/10.3390/arts3040350

Venter, O., Sanderson, E. W., Magrach, A., Allan, J. R., Beher, J., Jones, K. R., Possingham, H. P., Laurance, W. F., Wood, P., Fekete, B. M., Levy, M. A., &

Watson, J. E. M. (2016). Sixteen years of change in the global terrestrial human footprint and implications for biodiversity conservation. *Nature Communications*, *7*(1), 12558. https://doi.org/10.1038/ncomms12558

Yudelson, J., & Meyer, U. (2013). *The world's greenest buildings promise versus performance in sustainable design*. Routledge.

Zehir, M. A., Ortac, K. B., Gul, H., Batman, A., Aydin, Z., Portela, J. C., Soares, F. J., Bagriyanik, M., Kucuk, U., & Ozdemir, A. (2019). Development and field demonstration of a gamified residential demand management platform compatible with smart meters and building automation systems. *Energies*, *12*(5), 1–19. https://doi.org/10.3390/en12050913

CHAPTER 1

EDITORS' PREFACE

In the first chapter, Anne Cormier reformulates the discussion on measurements in architecture around the human body. She traces the history of the human body in architectural practice and discourse, highlighting their intricate connection even at the most minute scale. She questions some of the fundamentals of today's practices such as digitalization, standardization, and normalization. Highlighting that a scale-less architecture has no place for the human, that standards, in their aim to establish common values, actually exclude diversity, and that normalization reduces the range of possible solutions for our sustainability challenges restricting innovation. She proposes that today the exponential technological development, and the broad and competing scales of measurements relating to sustainability (from the micro-particles to global level) have rendered the scale of sustainable design infinite. She recommends to reconsider the *past* as a possible source for providing solutions for sustainability and to keep in mind the fundamentals of the discipline of architecture as a source for thoughtful inventiveness. Thus, while Cormier highlights that measurements of sustainability can be infinite, its meanings can only emerge by considering the human in the process of designing, building and occupying spaces – a notion that is fundamental to the history of the discipline.

Zoom-in, Zoom-out – Sustainability in the Scale(s) of Architecture

Anne Cormier
Université de Montréal

Sustainability in architecture is often confined to building materials and energy conservation. This chapter approaches sustainability from a broader architectural perspective. It offers a journey through the scales of architecture – from the human to the societal, and from the molecular to the urban. It exposes essential aspects of sustainability in architecture by exploring a series of questions. What are the dimensions of sustainability in architecture? How do they interact? Can they be counted or categorized? But most importantly, how do the architect and designer navigate across the multifaceted and intertwined scales of sustainability?

The fascinating vertigo that can be induced by the use of scale has been well depicted in Eva Szasz's (1968) *Cosmic Zoom*, and in Charles and Ray Eames' (1968) *A Rough Sketch for a Proposed Film Dealing with the Powers of Ten and the Relative Size of Things in the Universe*, produced the same year, and followed in 1977 by the seminal *Powers of Ten: A Film Dealing with the Relative Size of Things in the Universe and the Effect of Adding Another Zero* (Eames & Ray, 1977), both commissioned by IBM. The three short films were inspired by Kees Boeke's (1957) essay, *Cosmic View*. Zooming in and zooming out, the films expose the relative scale of humans to that of the universe. Today, zooming in and out on a computer screen has become a sort of nervous habit that blurs the very concept of scale in architecture.

In architecture, scale is primarily shrunk down. Most buildings have actual dimensions far too large to be drawn full size and printed on an easily transportable piece of paper. Scale has long been used as a tool to measure physical dimensions in order to verify design hypothesis and share information about buildings. The scale also allows one to situate a building within its environment, in relation to built structures, parks, rivers, and so on. Architects, builders and other professionals are still trained to read design and construction drawings at specific scales to understand what a building physically is, will be, was or could have been. A drawing's scale is part of what gives it legibility.

As of right now, and even despite the remarkable amount of data made available by information technologies, architectural working drawings, used by contractors to build, consist mainly of basic orthogonal projections of buildings' volumes: plans, sections and elevations. As Robin Evans explains in his essay on *Projective drawings* included in *Architecture and Its Image: Four Centuries of Architectural Representation* (Blau et al., 1989) these are truer to shape and dimensions than perspectives are. Although 3D digital modelling seems to be outmoding this standard, reading simple orthogonal projections gives one a wholesome, big-picture understanding of a building, which is particularly useful early on in the design process. With the exception of freehand sketches, these orthogonal projections are drawn at a precise scale or, in the digital world, without actual scale, but with the intention of being printed and read at a specific scale.

Scale gives a dimensional sense to drawings that makes them comprehensible to the naked eye. It brings, as Jean Zeitoun (1976) puts it, a fineness to a plan's legibility. Typically, the scales 1/16" = 1'-0", 1/8" = 1'-0", or 1/4" = 1'-0" (about 1:200, 1:100 and 1:50 in metric) are used to represent a whole building, or a major part of it, and interiors are drawn at ½"= 1'-0" (around 1:25). Details are drawn at 1"=1'-0", 3" = 1'-0" (close to 1:10 and to 1:5), and so on, up to 1" = 1" or 1:1, zooming in closer and closer to show materials and assemblage at full, handling size, scale. At all these scales, the relationship between the human body and the built environment is pictured effortlessly. With basic orthogonal drawings, it is easy to project oneself into the interior of a building. Notably, in the Imperial system, which is still used to measure construction material in some countries of the former British Empire, dimensions relate to body parts: the inch is about the width of a thumb, and a foot, the length of a foot. People often still use their feet as crude measuring tools, in fact.

This relationship of buildings to the human body—the white, male human body, to be frank—has long been the subject of theorization. For instance, in his treatise *De Architectura* Vitruvius investigated the subject of the human figure as the source of proportion. Leonardo da Vinci's famous *Vitruvian Man* drawing offers an interpretation of this ancient text and presents it as a microcosm of the world. In more recent times, Le Corbusier, criticizing both the metric system as *indifferent to the human measure*, and the Association française de normalisation (AFNOR), proposed *Le Modulor* as a new means of architectural normalisation based on human stature and mathematics. Even more recently, Alessandro Bosshard, Li Tavor, Matthew van der Ploeg, and Ani Vihervaara presented *Svizzeria 240: House Tour* at the 2018 Venice Biennale. The work, which received the Golden Lion, present the unfurnished interior of ordinary dwelling spaces which are built at unexpected scales in order to disconnect the human body from architecture and plunge visitors into an awkward, Carroll-esque wonderland.

Fundamental western architecture references, such as *Architectural Graphic Standards (AGS)*, first published in (Ramsey & Sleeper, 1932), and Ernst Neufert's *Bauentwurfslehre* (titled *Architect's Data* in its English version) which followed soon after in 1936, illustrate the extent to which establishing efficient relationships between the built environment and the human body became important over the course of the 20th century. Both books use anthropometric data (including reach, posture, and movement) to establish design standards, answering to the concept of normality, that are still broadly in use. Design have become embedded in norms and bylaws, both of which must be revised on a constant basis to satisfy ever-increasing demands for inclusivity. Architecture seeks to meet humans' physical needs, and yet most buildings are not built for just a single, specific person.

From a totally different perspective, the idea of the sheltering of the human body in a controlled environment has been the subject of critical projects such as Buckminster Fuller and Shoji Sadao's *Dome Over Manhattan* and François Dallégret's *Un-house, Transportable standard-of-living package*, both from the 1960s. At two very different scales – the projection of the dome in plan has a 2 mile (or 3,2 kilometer) diameter, and the horizontal diameter of the soft *un-house* bubble would be about 6 meters wide – these projects take a new stance on the living environment and propose asserting control over ambient air and conditioning it similarly to a submarine, or a plane. In both cases, the built form is essentially a limit between a protected inside and a potentially hostile outside. The two projects put forward a strategy of isolation.

More recently, turning the body's relationship to the world inside out, Georges Teyssot (2013) has proposed that cyborgs, by their very nature, are (or would be) environments:

> "Technology may not be integrated by 'imagining' a new environment, but perhaps by reconfiguring the body itself, pushing outward to where its artificial extremities encounter the 'world'. It is not so much a case of devising new dwellings for cyborgs. Those semi-human, semi-synthesized, constantly mutating entities are already environments, milieus, surfaces where relationship between self and world come into play. The cyborg thus entails a reconsideration of the body, literally (re)crafting it as an improved organism equipped with instruments, so that it can 'inhabit' the world and negotiate transactions with the multiple spheres of physical and mental comfort, media, and information" (Teyssot, 2013, pp 249-250).

His proposition suggests the redefinition of the interior of the dwelling "as the movement of the body toward the exterior, in a state of ek-stasis, through the various filters – thresholds, frontiers, wireless networks – that delimit our surroundings. It would be possible to turn inside-out the multiple surfaces that frame our 'place-of-being'. Like a Klein bottle – or an ordinary sock – the interior will conceivably be able to turn itself logically, and topologically, into an exterior. Architecture is thus transformed into a device that participates in this staging of an 'ecstasy'". (Teyssot, 2013, pp 249-250)

This interesting concept of inhabiting the world—however seductive, and comforting—is uneasy to grasp. Is it really about architecture? Or is it about something that architects might be able to conceive? The unknown re-crafted body it involves would generate new markers, and maybe new scales.

Meanwhile, at a scale foreign to architecture and to most of the building industry, the surreptitious invasion of the human body by components of the built form has become a scientifically verified fact. Toxic gases emanating from construction materials are often inhaled by inhabitants of buildings, and the effects of this have become a health issue. Resources such as the Healthy Building Network's Pharos Project, a database of chemicals, polymers, metals, and other substances, provide health and environmental information on common building products and on the certifications and standards used to measure the environmental and health impacts of building materials.

According to its website, the Pharos Project "profiles 101,392 chemicals and materials for 25 health and environmental hazards, including carcinogenicity, mutagenicity, reproductive toxicity and endocrine disruption, against 78 authoritative lists of hazards issued by governments, NGOs and other expert bodies [and] rates 347 product certifications and standards and uses them in building product evaluations" (Pharos Project, n.d.).

That the built environment can affect public health is not at all a new idea. The work of the Section d'hygiène urbaine et rurale du Musée Social, created in 1908 within the Le Playsian Parisian institution of the Musée Social[1], offers an example

---

[1] The Musée Social, now C.E.D.I.A.S (Centre d'Études, de Documentation, d'Information et d'Action Sociale), was upon its foundation the place where important research on social economy emerged as the moral and material betterment of the largest number of people without infringing the right to property and to the freedom of work. "l'amélioration morale et matérielle du sort du plus grand nombre, sans porter atteinte

of an organized group investigating exemplary urban projects as well as planning cities' transformation, construction and reconstruction in order to improve sanitary conditions[2]. The Section d'hygiène urbaine et rurale du Musée Social brought together, over 63 years of activity, a wide array of professionals, including administrators, architects, economists, geometers, historians, industrialists, journalists, lawyers, landscape architects, medical doctors, professors, and engineers.[3] The organization's research dealt with housing, workers gardens, open spaces, and nutrition. Its works and the lobby efforts of its members had a strong influence on the promotion of good hygienic practices as well as on the emergence of the pluridisciplinary field of urbanism, hygiene being approached primarily at the municipal level (Cormier, 1987).

The organization was strongly advocating the importance of open space, fresh air and sunlight, and, in order to favour the flow of air and natural light into the city and its homes. Eugène Hénard proposed, for instance, a project of *Boulevard à redans* that would introduce gardens open to the street in between Parisian street front façades, while Augustin Rey, with Justin Pidoux and Charles Barde, recommended the systematic orientation of buildings along a slightly skewed North-South axis...which today might be criticized as it might cause overheating.

A century or so later, the emergence of both new materials and the human capacity to investigate matter at a very small scale has expanded our physical relationship with buildings to encompass elements which are non-visible to the naked eye. Moreover, at a much broader scale, serious awareness of the multidimensional impact of the built environment on Earth's fragility has brought forth new considerations affecting architecture. These considerations include, besides good ventilation and direct sun penetration, factors such as efficiency of building envelopes, choice of materials (considering their performance, origin, composition, durability and eventual recycling), choice of structure and more astute handling of ambient air conditioning. This expansion of sustainability's definition has provoked quite a drastic changeover in architecture. In some instances, the constraint imposed by new design criteria seems to have justified an uninspired technocratic approach to building design.

---

au droit à la propriété et à la liberté du travail" (Procès verbaux du comité de direction du Musée Social, no 1, séance du 25 juin 1894).
[2] This work started with Paris, as the city's fortifications were being demolished, and continued with other cities including Alep, Barcelona, Damascus, Istanbul, Lille, Marseille, Ottawa, Philadelphia, Smyrna, and Tananarive.
[3] Amongst them, key figures such as Donat Alfred Agache, Jacques Marcel Auburtin, Gaston Bardet, Georges Benoit-Lévy, Louis Bonnier, Émile Cheysson, Raoul Dautry, Jean Claude Nicolas Forestier, Jacques Gréber, Eugène Hénard, Léon Jaussely, Marcel Poëte, Henri Prost, Augustin Rey, Georges Risler, Jules Siegfried, and Robert de Souza.

Conversely, these constraints have also brought architects, engineers, and clients to realise sophisticated projects.

Two University of British Columbia (UBC) buildings illustrate this point. A world of difference can be observed between UBC's first green architectural project, Matsuzaki Wright Architects' C.K. Choi building, which opened in 1996, and the Beaty Biodiversity Center, built on the same campus ten years later by Patkau Architects. The first project is an awkward assemblage of sustainable features that checks a list of criteria (such as those of the LEED) and, as a consequence, takes a myopic approach to sustainability. The second project possesses architecture that is overall remarkable, seeming to have seamlessly integrated the pursuit of sustainability. The Beaty Biodiversity Center appears to have been considered as a whole by its authors, they obviously have been zooming in and out from the scale of construction details, to the scale of its urban presence in the campus. Wouldn't it, therefore, be more sustainable?

The paradigm shift that the comprehension of human impact on Earth's future has brought on is happening alongside a complete digital transformation of the relationship architects have to drawings, and possibly to design and the built form. For instance, if the digital is greatly facilitating the capacity to generate non-orthogonal forms, it is also transforming the relationship to the tool of scale, as digital drawings are, in essence, without scale. One can zoom in and out on a screen and often draw regardless of scale. Understanding the specificity of various scales, once an indispensable practical and visual architectural ability, has now become bleary. Is this what *Svizzeria 240: House Tour* was ultimately all about?

This might be insignificant, and it might not. Nonetheless, the fact of the matter remains that a change in the relationship of architecture to its representation is occurring, and not only because of the lack of scale possessed by digital drawings, but also because certain software tools have replaced line weight (the thickness of a line, which is quite important to the legibility of a drawing) with colour-coding. This leads to a degree of abstraction that completely transforms the way a drawing, and therefore architecture, is read. Can a colour-code make the qualities of space as easily legible as line weight? Maybe.

Furthermore, the digital revolution has led to the development and implementation of productivity tools such as the Building Information Modeling (BIM), which is now claiming to model projects in 7D. Architectural intrusion into dimensions beyond the second and third has been proposed before. Sigfried Giedion's (1941) *Space, Time and Architecture: The Growth of a New Tradition* alludes to it, even adding a hyphen between *space* and *time* in *Space-time in art, architecture, and construction*, the book's Part VI. If space is understood in the Cartesian coordinate system, the meaning of time is broader. It refers to movement, with strong reference to Cubism and to contemporary architecture of the 1930s, but also to the timeless emotion that an artwork (including architecture) may convey.

BIM's four other dimensions, beyond 2D (orthogonal projections) and 3D (building form modelling), are: 4D scheduling, 5D estimating, 6D sustainability, and 7D facility management. Now, if 2D and 3D representations correlate with the form of a building itself – the spatial organisation of its program, its physical components, their dimensions and assemblage – the four new dimensions BIM introduces are of another nature entirely. With the possible exception of the sixth, these *dimensions* are data concerning the conditions of construction and maintenance of a building. Although they might be the dimensions of a process that will inevitably have an impact on a piece of architecture, by no means should they be considered literal dimensions of that architecture. Scheduling is obviously important but concerns the period that precedes a building's completion. Estimating, again, concerns the capacity to keep a project within the realm of affordability. And facility management deals with post-construction, but, really, for how many years is it possible to anticipate the conditions of facility management?

Furthermore, those introducing these *new dimensions* in what is presented as *modelling* should be doing so with caution. As James Utterback (2006) notes, a common criticism of CAD – and I would contend that BIM ends up actually being (mis)-used as a form of CAD early on in the design process instead of as a test-run preceding actual construction – is that it causes the designer to focus on details instead of the underlying principles of a project, which is antithetical to architectural design.

Returning quickly to BIM's sixth dimension, can sustainability be solely based on data regarding low-impact materials, energy efficiency, and durability and renewability, and afterlife of construction elements? Can data or building information modeling provide the essentially dimension of architecture that is timeless emotion? To ask the question is to answer it. But then again, timeless emotion might just be a romantic idea about architecture.

ON SCALES OF SUSTAINABILITY IN ARCHITECTURE

The word scale calls to mind the measurable—a measurable that is knowable. Sustainability, on the other hand, calls to mind something comprehendible more as a goal. The concept entails a great number of very diverse measurable elements that interact and interfere with one another and concern just about everything involved in attaining the goal of *sustainability*. In other words, one could say that the scales of sustainability are infinite. Given this, it is possible that we are totally clueless as far as genuinely attaining sustainability goes. However, this is likely not a reason to ignore what appears to be a quite urgent situation: the slow, agonizing extinction of life on Earth, a prospect that, though it may seem more distant than the planet's hypothetical mid-20th-century nuclear annihilation, may in fact be more real (Eken, 2017).

It is significant that the quest for both sustainability and digital expansion has been defining the reality of the 21st century up to now. One can hardly be addressed without, somehow, considering the other. Other unforeseen events, such as the COVID-19 pandemic, are now adding an unpredicted and dominating dimension to our reality. Besides creating a global crisis, such events are exacerbating digital communication and overshadowing the sustainability debate. Meanwhile, they expose vividly the valuable effects of the interruption of industrial and human activities on the environment, and put forward what is ultimately the main aim of sustainability: human survival and wellbeing.

This is not new. The paradigm of sustainability has however brought forward a better understanding of the conditions of our survival and wellbeing. It is however essential to not exclude from the array of scales of sustainability architecture's fundamental aim: a quest for timeless emotion, at however humble building scale that may be.

Architecture, which aims to house and enable human activity, is key in rethinking how human activity and development can take place without the devastating environmental impacts. At this point, the architecture and the way we design become one dimension that makes up the scales of sustainability – that define our relationship with the environment, our society and economy, for future generations to inherit.

REFERENCES

Blau, E., Kaufman, E., & Evans, R., & Centre Canadien d'Architecture. (1989). Architecture and its image : four centuries of architectural representation: works from the Collection of the Canadian centre for architecture. Centre Canadien d'Architecture (distributed by MIT Press).

Boeke, K. (1957). Cosmic view the universe in 40 jumps. J. Day.

Cormier, A. (1987), Extension, limites, espaces libres: Les travaux de la Section d'hygiène urbaine et rurale du Musée Social, Diplôme d'études approfondies, École d'architecture Paris-Villemin.

Eames, C., & Ray, E. (1968). A rough sketch for a proposed film dealing with the powers of ten and the relative size of things in the universe. IBM.

Eames, C., & Ray, E. (1977). *Powers of Ten*. Pyramid Films.

Eken, M. (2017, March). The understandable fear of nuclear weapons doesn't match reality. *The Conversation*. https://theconversation.com/the-understandable-fear-of-nuclear-weapons-doesnt-match-reality-73563

Giedion, S. (1941). Space, -time and architecture : the growth of a new tradition. Harvard University Press.

Neufert, E. (1936). *Bauentwurfslehre*. Bauwelt Werlag.

Pharos Project. (n.d.). *Search Pharos*. Retrieved April 22, 2020, from https://pharosproject.net/

Ramsey, C. G., & Sleeper, H. R. (1932). Architectural graphic standards for architects, engineers, decorators, builders and draftsmen. J. Wiley & Sons, Inc.; Chapman & Hall, Limited.

Szasz, E. (1968). *Cosmic Zoom*. National Film Board of Canada. http://www.nfb.ca/film/cosmic_zoom

Teyssot, G. (2013). A topology of everyday constellations. The MIT Press.

Utterback, J. M. (2006). *Design-inspired innovation*. World Scientific Publishing Co.

Zeitoun, J. (1976). La réduction du plan par l'effet d'échelle. In *Trames planes, Introduction à une étude architectuturale des trames* (pp. 31–39). Dunod.

CHAPTER 2

EDITORS' PREFACE

While Cormier hints that sustainability in architecture can be infinite and encompass more than measurements, Carmela Cucuzzella proposes to explore the other modes of *being* for sustainable architecture – beyond the quantitative dimension. She considers the question of what it means to *be* a sustainable architecture. She borrows Jean-Paul Sartre's work on existentialism – his three categories: being-in-itself, being-for-itself and being-for-others. She proposes to define the categories of being a sustainable architecture as facticity, potential and perception, respectively. By approaching sustainable architecture as a living entity, this essay unveils how it could fulfill its purpose across these three categories. Through this deconstruction, the essay demonstrates that most sustainable architecture is reduced to its facticity – from a discursive level. The essay brings forward the question of the possibility of being a sustainable architecture without fulfilling the three categories. By looking at examples of sustainable architecture that attempt to fulfill their purpose across the three categories and four pillars of sustainability (environmental, social, cultural and economic), the article proposes a matrix that could alternatively articulate quality for sustainable architecture. While many buildings aim to communicate *greenness* and thus are perceived as sustainable, without fulfilling their category of potential being (i.e., a sustainable building being for itself and that which it is not yet), these buildings could fail to meet long term sustainability goals. Even if sustainable architecture is fulfilling short-term expectations (what is perceived as sustainable today), the long-term goals require for its potential being to also be considered and designed.

Sustainable architecture as facticity, perception, and potential

Carmela Cucuzzella
Concordia University

INTRODUCTION

Architectural critique has always been an arduous task. Today, however, in the era of sustainable architecture and because of the overbearing pressures of environmental performance validation, it has become borderline impossible. The factual approach of assessing sustainable architecture makes it easier to understand how environmentally beneficial eco-friendly practices may be, but it also tends to leave central complex concerns of the project's embedded meaning at the periphery of its quality debate. If critique of sustainable architecture remains within the confines of that which can be measured, then only a small slice of the architecture qualities engendered by the concept can ever be assessed.

Thinking about sustainable architecture from the perspective of measurable eco-efficiency is inherently driven by a need for urgent solutions, one where eco-efficiency is the most promising strategy (Khasreen, Banfill, & Menzies, 2009). When eco-efficiency is the primary motivation behind designing sustainable architecture, then sustainable architecture remains within the realm of its facticity, perhaps at the expense of other more experiential, anticipative, or perceptual architectural qualities (Cucuzzella, 2015). I explore a specific ontological position that comprises three means of viewing sustainable architecture inspired by Jean-Paul Sartre's seminal work on existentialism: facticity (in-itself), potential (for-itself), and perceived (for-others). These three categories are considered in their capacity to engender sustainability differently, each with their specific means, and even scales, of conception. If we consider architecture as a living artefact, with a birth (its design intentions and construction), existence (occupancy phase), possible change of life (shifts in program or abandonment) and eventual end of life (demolition), then can we ask what is meant by *being* a sustainable architecture? In other words, what defines a sustainable architecture from an existential point of view?

Sustainability in architecture can span spatial scales, as well as temporal, cultural, and social scales. This chapter will focus on another notion of scales in sustainable architecture - that of the concept's ontology. Ontology here is primarily descriptive and classificatory in nature. I reflect on how the three existential categories by Sartre can elucidate the ontological scale of sustainable architecture.

WHAT IS MEANT BY 'BEING' SUSTAINABLE ARCHITECTURE?

In *Being and Nothingness*, a book with the subtitle, a Phenomenological Ontology, Jean-Paul Sartre describes and analyses two types of being: in-itself and for-itself, each having mutually exclusive characteristics (Sartre, 1993). Later in the book, Sartre adds a third ontology, *for-others,* because of our awareness of the 'other' as subject (Sartre, 1993). If we consider that phenomenology is based on the premise that reality consists of objects and events as they are perceived (Smith, 2008), then can we say that a phenomenological ontology is a descriptive account of being, not only from within, but also from without? Therefore, the *other* is an important component of existentialism.

The first category, being in-itself, represents objective facts. This is passive and inert. In the second category, being for-itself, Sartre claims that existence is that which is not. It is fluid and dynamic (Flynn, 2013). We can consider this to be potentiality. Therefore, being in-itself is facticity, while being for-itself is transcendence – a dichotomy of 'that which is' and 'that which can become'. Even if these two concepts are mutually exclusive, they are intimately related, just like past and future (Sartre, 1993). An entity's facticity directly influences its possibilities or its transcendence. Agency is essentially limited by the inadequate nature of its facticity.

However, being does not end at facticity and potential. The presence of others decentralizes and disrupts this dichotomy. According to Sartre, "The appearance of the Other in the world corresponds therefore to a fixed sliding of the whole universe, to a decentralization which I am simultaneously effecting" (Sartre, 1993, p.255). It is not only when others look, but the awareness that the other exists, that will enable an awareness of the self, experienced as an object for others. This third ontological category is that which is perceived. These ontological categories, as derived from the existential philosophy of Jean-Paul Sartre, are espoused for revealing what *being* a piece of sustainable architecture means: as facticity, as perceived and as potential. Perhaps two questions that can guide this study somewhat more pragmatically are these: In what manner are the three ontological stances of sustainable architecture manifest in the built form? And how can an understanding of these varying positions further the debates on what comprises sustainable architecture?

Let us briefly reflect on other categorizations of sustainable architecture in order to differentiate them from my proposed Sarterian one. For example, Simon Guy and Graham Farmer, in their article *Contested Constructions: competing logics of green buildings and ethics,* have identified six logics of sustainable architecture: ecological, smart, aesthetic, symbolic, comfort, and community, which are not mutually exclusive (Guy & Farmer, 2000). Each of these logics is characterized by a set of criteria: building image, risk, design strategy, rhetoric, scale, space, mobility, technology, etc. For example, in a smart perspective, the element that is at risk is the market survival, the design strategy is to reduce energy, the technology is hi-tech and intelligent, etc. In a symbolic logic, the element at risk is cultural life, the design strategy is contextual, the technology is low-tech and local, etc. Guy and Farmer's categories represent one set of many others available to delineate differing "issues that dominate the perception of an environmental dilemma" (Hajer, 1995, pp.19-20).

Indeed, if we compare the six competing logics identified by Guy and Farmer (2000) to those of Thomas Fisher (2008), the two sets are quite different from an ontological perspective and yet are both equally based on direct goals concerning issues of unsustainability. In *Architectural Design and Ethics*, Fisher (2008) proposes 14 principles to help the design community address issues related to sustainable development and diverge from the 'efficiency' model. Fisher's principles are somewhat similar to the 10 identified by One Planet Living[1], which range from the preventative (i.e., making a building more energy efficient by striving for zero carbon) to the more exploratory and prospective (i.e., encouraging active, sociable and meaningful lives). The Hannover Principles, as defined by William McDonough Architects, are based on the idea that humans and nature must coexist (William McDonough Architects, 1992). Sim Van Der Ryn and Stuart Cowan's (2007) five principles of ecological design focus on the environmental pillar by adopting a vision of contextual, passive, integrated design that comprises didactic elements for learning. And these are just a few examples developed in the past three decades. A Sarterian lens, on the other hand, is entirely different. It moves beyond the content goals of sustainability and into a perspective encompassing a project's existence and essence – something that may have been lost in the rush towards eco-efficiency aims in sustainable building design.

Sartre's inquiry into the core of human existence, through the categories of in-itself, for-itself and for-others, can be redirected to question *what it means to be* sustainable architecture. If we consider that choice is made possible through a series of inquiries, let us elaborate some more on the analogy between human choice to create meaning in life and design inquiry to create meaning in sustainable architecture. If we consider Sartre's three existential categories as a means to develop different forms of design inquiry towards sustainable architecture, then this can help structure how architecture defines its own meaning. For example, if we explore the methods of design evaluation and judgement for sustainable architecture, we quickly realize that these three categories provide distinctly different design options and outcomes. Specifically, the facticity dimension would focus on *the evidence* of the building's eco-efficiency. The potential dimension would focus on *anticipatory narratives* providing meaningful ways forward

---

[1] The set of these principles are defined on URL=http://www.oneplanetliving.org

Sustainable architecture as facticity

regarding sustainability. The perception dimension would focus on the *legibility* of the eco-constructive choices apparent to others. Table 2.1 takes a closer look at Sartre's facticity, potential and perception and suggests an ontology of what each category signifies for sustainable architectural design.

Table 2.1 General distinction between facticity, potentiality, and perception as means for sustainable architectural design inquiry

	Facticity as Design Inquiry	Potentiality as Design Inquiry	Perception as Design Inquiry
Design evaluation based on	Optimization – evidence of eco-performance efficiency	Exploration – generating anticipatory narratives with broad ideas of sustainability	Legibility – ensuring eco-constructive choices
Construction of knowledge	Objectively	Imaginatively	Normatively
Types of uncertainty	Technical and methodological (data unavailability, method inadequacies)	Epistemological (indeterminate)	Perceptibility (unreadability/ambivalence of eco-features)
Type of consequences considered	Predictable, measurable	Prospective, anticipative	clarity of eco-messages conveyed
Elements of concern (risks)	Resource/planet preservation, social-economic fairness, and cost-benefit analysis (objective and measurable)	Ecological integrity, social cohesion, place identity/memory, cultural/community life, (ethical and aesthetic)	Delivery of eco-messages and responsible choices taken (visible and non-visible)
Temporal perspective	Short-term thinking	Long-term thinking	Short-term thinking
Spatial perspective	Functional and flexible	Organic, fluid, context specific, tactile, sensory, experiential	Demonstrative and legible
Type of innovation	Technical innovation (performance/efficiency)	Multi-faceted innovation (ethical/aesthetical)	Communication innovation of eco-design features
Design strategy	Reduction and optimization: energy, footprint, social injustice, resources	Narrative and symbolic: contextual, identity, community, cultural revitalization, environmental regeneration	Expressive and legible: demonstrate eco-efficiency, reveal eco-performance through constructive choices
Methodology for design inquiry	Systematic thinking (LCA, SLCA, EIA, SIA, LEED, Ecological Footprint)	Prospective, anticipative, (exploratory approaches, experiential, aesthetic)	Communicative design to expose qualitative and quantitative results of eco-features

Notes: ©Cucuzzella, 2019

A Sarterian lens then provides a means to reflect beyond the technically quantifiable goals of a given project's sustainability (its facticity) and to adopt a perspective including that project's existence and essence. Sartre's existential categories of facticity, potential and perception, translated into a set of ontological scales, can contribute to the clarification of a project's *reason for being* sustainable architecture as a whole, rather than through its eco-characteristics alone. The next sections demonstrate this through a series of examples.

Sustainable Architecture as Facticity (In-itself)

Facticity constitutes the *givens* of a situation. Why is facticity so important in sustainable design? If we consider a project's facticity as the given set of facts precisely describing its attributes, then its facticity can be used to prove the benefits it affords its environment. I maintain that sustainable architecture *as facticity* refers to an architecture whose eco-efficient, socio-beneficial building characteristics are objectively measurable. Facticity refers to sustainable architecture *in-itself* – as an object of measurable performance. This may refer to the performance measures of the building's material and production choices, how it is engineered, metrics related to its structure, water system, and energy efficiencies, air and light, among other physical facts of built form. These considerations are of obvious necessity but prove limited as a universal criterion for assessing sustainable architecture. Furthermore, what can be said about the certainty that is attributed to the facticity of sustainable architecture? John Dewey, in *The Quest for Certainty, a Study of the Relation of Knowledge and Action*, first published in 1930 saw this quest of certainty in facts and knowledge as a means towards freedom:

> "Men readily persuade themselves that they are devoted to intellectual certainty for its own sake. Actually, they want it because of its bearing on safeguarding what they desire and esteem. The need for protection and prosperity in action created the need for warranting the validity of intellectual beliefs" (Dewey, 1990, pp.40-41).

Dewey suggests that the certainty humans have attributed to quantified results is a way for them to be able to justify their own desires. In this way, the facticity of a sustainable architectural project 'safeguards' its environmental imperatives as well as the efforts made to include, for example, best-practice eco-technologies, all in the effort to reduce environmental risks. In the process, eco-technologies, and the ease with which measurements can be extracted for ensuring their performance promises, have come to dominate the profession of sustainable architecture (Boecker et al., 2009; Farmer, 1996; Tabb & Senem Deviren, 2014; Wines, 2000). About 30 years after Dewey's publication on *The Quest for Certainty*, Jacques Ellul wrote an entire book on the technological society, and specifically how technology has come to drive individual intention. He explains that:

> "(...) the individual participates only to the degree that he is subordinate to the search for efficiency, to the degree that he resists all the currents today considered secondary, such as aesthetics, ethics, fantasy. Insofar as the individual represents this abstract tendency, he is permitted to participate in the technical creation, which is increasingly independent of him and increasingly linked to its own mathematical law" (Ellul, 1964, p.74)

There is, however, a circular paradox of risk assessment. Modern understanding of the consequences of technologies is supposed to help us better assess the occurrence of environmental risks. Indeed, Anthony Giddens (2004) has stated that the modern understanding of risk was supposed to help humans control and normalize their future. However, according to Giddens (2004) and Beck (2004), things have not turned out that way, and our attempts to control the future have in fact led to the realization that humans need different methods for contending with risk.

If pure facticity refers to full positivity, it is fragmented information and incomplete in its capacity to allow an understanding of a complex, whole entity. As an object represented by its measurable performance, sustainable architecture *in-itself*, focuses on the 'what is'. There is little attention on the 'what can be' as an architecture with potentiality. One can find many examples from around the world whose facticity is the basis for an essence of sustainable architecture.

The first example, the Bibliothèque du Boisé (Library of the Woods) in the municipality of Saint-Laurent in Montreal was completed in 2013. It is a LEED-platinum certified library (Figure 2.1). The building is the result of an architecture competition where the designers' submission was embedded in a high degree of facticity. A quote from the competition submission explains the sustainable characteristics of the library:

> "Several strategies are then put in place, they are present throughout the process of discovery, appropriation, and progression, from the landscape to the book. At the scale of the site, the strengthening of the vegetal environment, the reservoirs of water retention expressed and highlighted, the responsible parking and the related facilities set up the basic premises. The building's own materiality contributes greatly to the understanding of an exceptional building, but it is mainly through its mechanical systems that it will innovate. The establishment of a system for the recovery of rainwater and its serving of the botanical environment, a geothermal system connected to a heat exchange loop, various measures of energy saving etc... But principally, the introduction of a passive heating system, which uses the heat accumulated within the glass prism and redistributed within the geothermal loop" (Cardinal Hardy et al., 2009, p.3-4[2])

---

[2] Translated by author

Figure 2.1 Bibliothèque du Boisé. St. Laurent, Montreal, Canada - 2014

Notes:
- (left) front entrance exterior stairs; (right) white reflective interior central skylight
- by Labonté Marcil, Cardinal Hardy, Eric Pelletier architectes
- Photos © Cucuzzella

The designers of the Bibliothèque du Boisé relied heavily on technological systems to accommodate the building's sustainable characteristics, thus offering evidence that their vision of sustainability was based on facticity. They focused on the amalgamation of best-practice eco-technologies rather than on creating an overall vision or meaning through/of/for sustainability. The setting of the project, situated along a wide-spanning highway in the north part of the city, was ripe for fresh ideas. The site of the library is a barren highway, difficult to access, and unwelcoming in its urban context. The building is monumental, adding to the unwelcoming characteristic of the site, and includes a plethora of best-practice technologies. Neither is innovative, especially for this context. The link between ethic (the imperative to provide a better place to live for society) and poetics (the architect's desire for an eloquent place to live) is what true architecture is according to Alberto Pérez-Gómez (2006). The Bibliothèque succeeded in confirming its *being sustainable architecture* through its facticity, but at what cost?

A second example illustrates how sustainable architecture can move beyond facticity, yet is *perceived* (for-others) as sustainable and has *potential* (for-itself) beyond that which is measurable (in-itself). The Centre for Sustainable Energy Technologies of the University of Nottingham's campus in Ningbo was built in 2008 (Figure 2.2). It is commonly described in terms of its broad range of best-practice environmental technologies included to help reduce energy use, increase daylight, and provide natural ventilation, in addition to many other environmental features with very precise measurable eco-benefits. Even though it was the first zero carbon building in China and was designed specifically with showcasing its environmental technologies and sustainable construction in mind, the building's spectacular sculptural character, depicting a Chinese lantern, alludes to local cultural references, giving it a distinct spirit.

Sustainable architecture as facticity 31

The main architect of the building, Mario Cucinella, believes that pieces of sustainable architecture can have multi-faceted purposes. In a book entitled, *Behind the Green Door*, he quotes:

> "Each building can have a positive impact on the regeneration of the surrounding environment. Green buildings with a design reflecting local culture, and the capacity of meeting resource demands with renewables, can reduce inequalities in the access to essential services and create a new space for socio-economic interaction. This means that it is possible to extend our responsibility to an unlimited area" Mario Cucinella in (Rotor, 2014, p. 69).

Figure 2.2 The Centre for Sustainable Energy Technologies. Ningbo, China - 2008

Notes:
- (left) exterior side view; (right) evening view
- by Mario Cucinella Architects

The form of the Centre for Sustainable Energy Technologies refers to a Chinese lantern. Can this key cultural depiction of Chinese culture be considered socially sustainable in its aim to evoke Chinese symbolism? Since the lantern symbolizes community booming life and prosperous business to the Chinese, the interaction that such a building has with its site and people provides great possibilities, both real and imaginary. In this way, it is sustainable architecture as *potential*.

"(…) the striped glass façade was inspired by traditional Chinese lanterns and fans. However, the main purpose of the design was to showcase technologies for energy efficient climate control" Mario Cucinella in Archello.com. [3]

Furthermore, the Centre's host of visible eco-features provides the perception of environmental sustainability. This characteristic demonstrates sustainable architecture as *perceived*. Unlike the Bibliothèque du Boisé, which failed to provide an architecture beyond its facticity, this building by Mario Cucinella represents sustainable architecture well beyond its facticity.

Sustainable Architecture as Potential (For-itself)

Sustainable architecture *as potential* refers to that which the building aims to become – not only as it is *in-itself* as a set of facts (facticity), not only how it is seen and identified *for-others* (perception), but also, what it has the possibility to become, *for-itself*. It refers to a building's transcendence, its ability to live up to a designer's intentions, its set of desired experiences (sensorial or otherwise), and its multiple designed functions. A piece of architecture, considered in terms of its *potential*, begins to evolve from a newly erected structure to a continually changing entity, from its originally intended design to a completely different experience.

Some examples of this type of architecture could include exterior spaces that collapse to become interior spaces, a structure that grows organically over time to accommodate different programs, or a building envelope that becomes a broadcasting device. Architecture as potential 'goes beyond' simple facticity yet includes quantifiable properties (facts about the building) and emerges in light of their *possibility*. This possibility is not a function of ad hoc forces, but rather one of the architecture's intentions, that is known for its specific context and situation. A piece of architecture's potentiality can be understood as a seed embedded within its facticity that aims to produce specific outcomes. A sustainable piece of architecture is therefore co-constituted by what it is (its facticity) and what it is intended to achieve (its potential), both of which are embedded in its existence.

There are many instances of sustainable architecture that cannot be perceived as sustainable simply because its eco-features are not exhibited. If a building cannot be *perceived* as sustainable, that does not imply that it is not sustainable. For example, the Médiathèque François Villon, built in 2014 in Bourg-la-Reine, France, and designed by Pascale Guédot is a project with a small ecological

---

[3] Retrieved on April 24, 2020 from https://archello.com/project/centre-for-sustainable-energy-technologies#story-1

footprint and a delicate architectural expression (Figure 2.3). It incorporates a restrained, yet effective selection of technologies to improve energy efficiency and conserve water. For example, it is equipped with a rainwater collection system, reinforced thermal insulation, and a geothermal heat pump for heating and cooling. The building is HQE (Haute Qualité Environnementale) certified. Abundant natural light enters through the glass façade and a large skylight allows the diffusion of light without overheating the library.

Figure 2.3 Médiathèque François Villon. Bourg-la-Reine, France - 2014

Notes:
- (left) salvaged tree, (right) view from interior and its connection to the exterior
- by Pascale Guédot

How this architecture expresses its environmental consciousness stands in stark contrast to other eco-technological projects. The project does not flaunt any visible eco-technologies, even if it is effectively environmentally sustainable. This represents the building's strength and works as a prime example of how it is not necessary that ecological correctness be "accompanied by a sour puritanical expression, as if something has to taste bitter in order to do us good" (Sauerbruch & Hutton, 2011, p.48). The visual, spatial and constructive characteristics of sustainable buildings all tell a story and become key to those buildings' successful introduction to communities. An architecture's *potential* is not only tightly related to its *facticity*, but also to its *perception*.

The Ningbo History Museum in Zhejiang, China, built in 2008, is a piece of sustainable architecture that stands apart from the canon of high-tech eco-buildings (Figure 2.4). Its design is not an exercise of eco-optimization, as in the category of sustainable architecture as facticity, nor is it an architecture of eco-messages that comprises visible eco-technologies, as in the category of sustainable architecture as perception. Rather, it is a design that critiques the site of the museum itself. Wang Shu, of *Amateur Architecture*, Pritzker Prize winner in 2012, and the project's designer, has explained his process:

"When I designed this, I was thinking of mountains. I couldn't design something for the city, because there is no city here yet, so I wanted to do something that had life. Finally, I decided to design a mountain. It's a part of Chinese tradition" (Wang Shu, 2012)[4].

Figure 2.4 Ningbo History Museum. Ningbo, Zhejiang, China - 2008

Notes:
- (left) street view, (right) its façade
- by Amateur Architecture Studio

The museum's most striking feature is its façade (Figure 2.4, right image), which comprises a variety of earthy-coloured bricks, stones and tiles, all taken from the ruins of demolished villages in the area. Wang Shu's museum is intended to encourage visitors to reflect on the changes occurring in the area. First, it allows visitors to think of the massive demolition that has taken place. Second, the design helps to reflect on the promises that future development brings while still keeping the memory of the original villages alive. In this way, the Ningbo Museum is sustainable architecture *as potential*. It gives a second life to the considerable debris left behind by the rapid new development of the area, resurfacing memories of a bygone era. The building itself represents life to Wang Shu, with the symbolism of the mountain representing a seed for renewed life. Its *potential* is also revealed as a museum intended to inspire architects to think about sustainability in very divergent ways, planting seeds in their minds and moving far beyond sustainable architecture as facticity. The architecture therefore has the potential both to make its viewers think about its destructive past and to provide hope for future urban prosperity. This is an

---

[4] Wang Shu in Brendan McGetrick's article entitled, *Ningbo History Museum*, *Domus*, March 3, 2012, https://www.domusweb.it/en/from-the-archive/2012/03/03/ningbo-history-museum.html.

exemplar of sustainable architecture for-itself – an architecture with a conscious potentiality.

The SOF Danish National Maritime Museum in Helsingør, built in 2013 and designed by BIG, is an example that can help explain the *potential* of an industrial ruin — of an abandoned shipping dock, more specifically (Figure 2.5). The museum is located in front of the Kronborg Castle, but its placement is very discreet. Repurposing the abandoned, boat-shaped dry dock mentioned above, it is built entirely underground and surrounded by a concrete structure. This is intended to keep the vistas to the castle clear and ensure that its historic walls remain undisturbed. Bjarke Ingels explains the project development:

> "Leaving the 60-year-old dock walls untouched, the galleries are placed below ground and arranged in a continuous loop around the dry dock walls – making the dock the centerpiece of the exhibition – an open, outdoor are where visitors experience the scale of ship building" (BIG-Bjarke Ingels Group, 2017) [5].

Figure 2.5 SOF - Danish National Maritime Museum. Helsingør, Denmark - 2013

Notes:
- (left) evening view, (right) view of bridge
- by Bjarke Ingels Group: BIG

The empty dock, which is at the center of the museum, has been converted into a public courtyard where visitors can experience the scale of the ship building. The museum, thus, is a *sustainable building for-itself* since it aims to preserve its historical essence in its new life, with a capacity to preserve the imaginary of its past. The dock provides the foundation of the museum, while the museum becomes an inhabited ruin that preserves the dock's shipbuilding history. Making the site's historical meaning the centre of the museum's design narrative is a conscious means of maintaining the memory of a place in order

---

[5] BIG-Bjarke Ingels Group, Inexhibit (blog), November 25, 2017, https://www.inexhibit.com/case-studies/danishnational-maritime-museum/.

to build its future. The designers' need to structure their building in this manner is potentiality. It is being for-itself. It is neither random nor neutral. It is conscious(ness).

Sustainable Architecture as Perception (For-others)

If we consider the third category of *being* sustainable architecture as that which can be *perceived*, then what is of interest are the apparent sustainable features. Sustainable architecture *as perceived* refers to that which is seen, discernible, expressed, or even experienced. In adopting Sartre's terms, it is architecture 'for-others'. For example, abundant natural daylighting, lavish vegetation on walls, solar panels on building envelopes, among other recognizable qualities, can all be categorized as characteristics that allow the perception of sustainability. Including such recognizable qualities in a building allows patrons or even the public to perceive the building as one that is respectful of its environment.

The perception of sustainability, in some contexts, may be as important as the facticity of an architecture. Climate change and the promises of mitigation or prevention have become prominent marketing opportunities today (Hansen & Manchin, 2009). They allow owners of a visibly sustainable building, public or private, to communicate that they are stewards of the planet. However, the terms greenwashing or green-sheen, which have emerged in the past several decades, refer to the deceptive ways that the green agenda can be spun into a product or building's narrative. This is the case when the perception of sustainability does not translate into actual sustainable architecture. In other words, if the perception of sustainable architecture does not match its facticity, it may lead to deceptive claims.

Sustainable architecture, *as perceived*, is vital when it aims to distinguish itself from other architectures that are not or do not appear to be sustainable. The visible eco-features included in a building are semantically significant. They provide purposeful meaning. This symbolism may or may not be part of an overall storyline. The denotation of sustainable characteristics, however, may lead to the connotation of stewardship and responsibility, as well as a healthier building, among other morally positive qualities. Indeed, sustainable-looking physical characteristics may lead to layers upon layers of meanings and even myths that have come to be widely accepted (Barthes, 1972, 1977). For instance, the (Barthes, 1972, 1977) perception of the green roof and how it has been accepted as a responsible design feature, is a prime example of a contemporary myth. It is perceived as an environmental imperative because it is understood to provide increased insulation, green space, diversity of plant species, and fresh air, among other symbols of environmentalism. Yet little attention is ever given to how poorly green roofs actually provide such benefits in Nordic countries. The power of the myth of the green roof is key for the perception of a sustainable architecture to hold as true. Is the green roof so embedded in popular culture and so highly mythicized as a universal environmental solution that it hides in its own mystifications? In his seminal book *Mythologies*, Roland Barthes writes the following:

> "The unveiling which it [myth] carries out is therefore a political act: founded on a responsible idea of language, mythology thereby postulates the freedom of the latter. It is certain that in this sense mythology *harmonizes* [emphasis added] with the world, not as it is, but as it wants to create itself" (Barthes, 1972, p. 156).[6]

In the above case, the connotation of a green roof is associated with the myth of stewardship, only until the myth is debunked. Has the mythicization of visible eco-features come to be more culturally significant than those features' measurable performance? Seattle's Ballard Library, built in 2005, acts as a deliberate showcase of environmental features (Figure 2.6). The team went to great lengths to make the green roof visible, not only from above, but also from below. A small windowed room protrudes from the roof to give visitors a panoramic view of the green roof, where a periscope was built into one of the walls to allow viewing from the lobby. A row of photovoltaic panels on the roof also serves as an educational tool, though it does not provide energy for the operation of the building. The patrons of the library do not have access to the roof. They can only observe it. The messages conveyed by the library's eco-features express environmental stewardship and have come to be widely accepted myths of their time. They are clear because the symbolism embedded in the eco-features has come to be widely accepted (Umberto, 1997).

What is important to highlight is that the messages delivered through the eco-features will be read and understood very differently in 5 or 10 years. These symbols represent a language with an expiry date. Barthes (1972) has said that "language is never innocent". For Barthes, "the myth-consumer takes the signification for a system of facts; myth is read as a factual system, whereas it is but a semiological system" (Barthes, 1972, p. 131).

---

[6] Highlight Roland Barthes

Figure 2.6 Ballard Library. Seattle, Washington - 2013

Notes:
- (left) side view, (right) green roof
- by Bohlin Cywinski Jackson

We know that this practice of *sustainable architecture as perception* can be deceptive, but can it ever be productive? In *Taking Shape*, Susannah Hagan argues that aesthetics could contribute to environmental architecture since making visible brings forward what is suppressed, lost or emergent (Hagan, 2001). She claims that visibility accelerates the emergence and awareness of environmental concerns. Sang Lee, in his edited book entitled *Aesthetics of Sustainable Architecture*, maintains that "[a]esthetics of architecture refers to the expressions in built form that closely relate to the way in which the form is not only conceived but also produced in relation to a certain purpose and its context" (Lee, 2011, p.11). Lee goes on to say that,

> "(…) if a building or an environment is designed and built to be sustainable, it should inform how it was conceived and situated, and what makes it be so under what kind of conditions. And in the presence of such a work, it should be perceivable and or understandable that it serves and fits such purpose" (Lee, 2011, p. 11)

This type of architectural expression has a purpose – to raise environmental consciousness for which the ideas of sustainability and durability are key (Lee, 2011). The difference between sustainability and durability is that the former is the ability to maintain and support a system, ideally indefinitely. The latter is about the state of an object and its ability to function for a specific time intended (or longer). It is important to highlight that there is a fine line between greenwashing and productive eco-visibility, although its reflection is beyond the scope of this chapter.

The Water and Life Museums complex in Hemet, California, completed in 2008, was the first building of its type (museum) to obtain a LEED Platinum certification. It is an example of a building whose perception of sustainability is key, since the purpose of its exhibits is to provide information about the preservation of local resources. The building is a 'living' example of resource conservation (Figure 2.7). Harnessing the desert sun, the museum's roofs are completely covered with photovoltaic panels, producing energy while protecting the interior from the hot sun. The 3,000 solar panels generate fifty percent of the museums' energy. The two loggias between the museums feature special, semi-transparent photovoltaic panels that provide some shade as well as energy. This example's perception of sustainability is coupled tightly with its facticity, since its eco-features not only convey messages of responsibility, but also provide significant resource savings, even in a site as harsh as Hemet's arid desert.

Figure 2.7 Water and Life Museum complex. Hemet, California - 2008

Notes:
- (left) top view, (right) the solar array
- by Lehrer Architects, Gangi Architects

Sustainable architecture as perception is therefore a core component of the Water and Life Museum. Given the urgent nature of climate change, it seems understandable that architects would rely on creative responses that clearly showcase their sustainability. Reliance on perception alone, however, without a matching facticity, can be counterproductive to both, attaining a building's ecological goals and contributing to the global shift towards more sustainable development strategies. Today, one could even posit that sustainable architecture is so concerned with its perception that it tends towards a type of eco-didacticism, where the building becomes a political means of expression. Jacques Ranciere, in *The Politics of Aesthetics* claims that,

> "Politics and art, like forms of knowledge, construct 'fictions', that is to say material rearrangement of signs and images, relationships between what is seen and what is said, between what is done and what can be done" (Ranciere, 2011[2000], p.39).

The limitation is that unless the audience of a work is conscious of the politics (or intended messages) of the piece, then the conversation between the viewer and the piece can never take place. Ranciere goes on to suggest that:

> "[T]here are politics of art that are perfectly identifiable. It is thoroughly possible to single out the form of politization at work in a novel, a film, a painting, an installation, or a building. If this politics coincides with an act of constructing political dissensus, this is something that the art in question does not control" (Ranciere, 2011[2000], p.62)

In addition to conceptions of facticity (in-itself) and perception (for-others), there exists also a type of sustainable architecture whose potential extends beyond its brick and mortar and to a place where sustainable architecture can become that which it is not yet. What does this suggest?

CONCLUDING REFLECTIONS

In the previous sections, a series of architectural examples helped us investigate and appreciate three ontological scales of sustainable architecture: *facticity*, *potential*, and *perception*. This exploration was founded on the hypothesis that facticity is the most widespread means of creating sustainable architecture, while potentiality seems to be the least. Sustainable architecture as perception appears to be a strategic means, allowing for a particular reading whenever necessary.

This investigation of what it means to be a sustainable architecture through the Sarterian existential lens has contributed to the structuring of how sustainable architecture can define its own meaning through different forms of design inquiry. Table 2.1 (above) defines the ontology of what each of these scales signifies for design inquiry. As a further synoptic exercise, we have implemented the design inquiry categories of Table 2.1 to envision an arbitrary sustainable architecture project. It is obvious that numerous outcomes are possible through this preliminary design thinking exercise, so the table is not intended as a final list of questions. Its aim is to unveil the applicability of our three ontological scales when thinking about the essence of, or its reason for being, a sustainable architecture project. The results of the exercise are shown in Table 2.2.

The premises and inquiries presented in Table 2.2 depict the vast differences between how each ontological category treats sustainable architecture. In the facticity (in itself) category, the green building is an instrumental object; in the potential (for itself) category, the sustainable architecture becomes a means to other ends, in the perception (for others) category, the architecture is an exercise of demonstration.

Table 2.2 Examples of concerns within ontological categories of facticity, potential, and perception for a sustainable architecture project

Spheres of Concern → Onto-logical Inquiry ↓	Economic addressing individual and organizational economic development	Environmental addressing resource depletion, environmental damages and regeneration	Social addressing social coherence, community life and individual comfort	Cultural addressing symbolism, contextual significance, heritage, and cultural diversity
Facticity (in-itself)	The green building as a form of organizational growth. How can we make a profit with the building by making it efficient?	The green building as a way to optimize performance while reducing impacts. How can we reduce the negative environmental impacts of the building?	The green building as a way to increase local business opportunity (socio-economic). How can we reduce the negative social repercussions while constructing the building?	The green building seen as a way to increase local tourism (cultural-economic). How can we increase the number of people visiting the building?
Potential (for-itself)	The architectural project as means for organizational and community development. How can the ecological strategy be economically fecund? Does the building help economically develop the community?	The architectural project as means for environmental regeneration. How can we offset the negative environmental effects of the building? Have passive or contextual solutions been properly considered?	The architectural project as means for enhancing community life. Does it contribute to the social regeneration of the community? Is the functional dimension flexible enough to ensure a second life to the building?	The architectural project as means for cultural impetus. How can we ensure that the cultural diversity and the contextual significance of place are enriched? Does this artifact provide a cultural impetus for the community?
Perception (for-others)	The architectural project as an eco-economic exemplar. How can the building appear to be economically viable? How do the technologies adopted show that they contribute to the economic development of the community?	The architectural project as an visibly green building. How can we showcase all the environmental features to show the public our responsible choices? How can we show that we are sustaining not only our species but all species?	The architectural project as a means to show the importance of social cohesion and equity. How can we show that the social repercussions are equitable? How can the building demonstrate that it contributes to the social regeneration?	The architectural project as a means to further popularize the environmental culture. How can we show that the contextual significance of place are readable to the public? Does this building enrich the environmental culture for the community?

Notes: ©Cucuzzella, 2019

As a final thought experiment, if the radical dualism of Sartre's in-itself (its facticity) and for-itself (its potential) categories is encapsulated in a sustainable architecture project, as shown through the set of inquiries of Table 2.1 and Table 2.2, it would not just be eco-productive. It would also have the potential to make great contributions to society, to culture, to the environment and even possibly to the economy. This would represent a great leap forward, given that, in current practice, the rush to prove sustainable architecture's ability to reduce environmental impacts has, for the most part, been drastically relegated to the realm of facticity. If a purely facticity-focused approach can be complemented by the consideration of the other (its perception), which also can help build a culture of sustainability, then can this Sarterian framework help make clear the definition of quality in sustainable architecture today?

REFERENCES

Barthes, R. (1972). *Mythologies*. Paladin.

Barthes, R. (1977). Rhetoric of the Image. In S. Heath (Ed.), *Image-Music-Text* (pp. 32-51). Hill and Wang.

Beck, U. (2004). *Risk Society: Towards a New Modernity* (R. Mark, Trans.). Sage.

Boecker, J., Horst, S., Keiter, T., Lau, A., Sheffer, M., Toevs, B., & Reed, B. (2009). *The Integrative Design Guide to Green Building - Redefining the Practice of Sustainability*. John Wiley & Sons, Inc.

Hardy, Labonté Marcil, Eric Pelletier architectes en consortium, LBHA, SDK, & TEKNIKA·HBA. (2009). *Saint-Laurent Library competition: Un trait de paysage dans la ville*. In Saint Laurent Library 2009 Architectural Competition, Phase 2. City of Montreal.

Cucuzzella, C. (2015). Judging in a World of Expertise: When the Sum of the Parts is LESS than the Whole. In J.-P. Chupin, C. Cucuzzella, & B. Helal (Eds.), *Architecture Competitions and the Production of Culture, Quality and Knowledge: An International Inquiry* (pp. 144-161). Potential Architecture Books.

Dewey, J. (1990). *The Quest for Certainty - A Study of the Relation of Knowledge and Action*. George Allen & Unwin Ltd (first published in 1930).

Ellul, J. (1964). *The Technological Society* (J. Wilkinson, Trans. original version in French, 1954 ed.). Vintage Books.

Farmer, J. (1996). *Green Shift: Towards a green sensibility in architecture*. Butterworth Architecture in association with WWF-UK.

Fisher, T. (2008). *Architectural Design and Ethics: Tools for Survival*. Elsevier/Architectural Press.

Flynn, T. (2013). Jean-Paul Sartre. *The Stanford Encyclopedia of Philosophy*. Fall 2013 Edition. Retrieved from <https://plato.stanford.edu/archives/fall2013/entries/sartre/>

Giddens, A. (2004). *Modernity and Self-Identity: Self and Society in the Late Modern Age*. Polity Press and Blackwell Publishing (first edition 1991).

Guy, S., & Farmer, G. (2000). Contested Constructions: The Competing Logics of Green Buildings and Ethics. In W. Fox (Ed.), *Ethics and the Built Environment* (pp. 73-87). Routledge.

Hagan, S. (2001). Taking Shape: A new cultural contract between architecture and nature. Architectural Press.

Hajer, M. (1995). The Politics of Environmental Discourse: Ecological Modernization and the Policy Process. Oxford University Press.

Hansen, A., & Manchin, D. (2009). Visually Branding the Environment: Climate Change as a Marketing Opportunity. *Discourse Studies, 10*(6), 777-794.

Khasreen, M. M., Banfill, P. F. G., & Menzies, G. F. (2009). Life-Cycle Assessment and the Environmental Impact of Buildings: A Review. *Sustainability (Switzerland), 1*, 674-701. doi:10.3390/su1030674

Lee, S. (Ed.) (2011). *Aesthetics of Sustainable Architecture*. 010 Publishers.

Pérez-Gómez, A. (2006). Built Upon Love: Architectural Longing after Ethics and Aesthetics. MIT Press.

Ranciere, J. (2011[2000]). *The Politics of Aesthetics: The Distribution of the Sensible* (G. Rockhill, Trans.). Continuum.

Rotor. (2014). Behind the Green Door: A Critical Look at Sustainable Architecture through 600 Objects. Oslo Architecture Triennale.

Sartre, J.-P. (1993). *Being and Nothingness*. Washington Square Press.

Sauerbruch, M., & Hutton, L. (2011). What Does Sustainability Look Like? In S. Lee (Ed.), *Aesthetics of Sustainable Architecture*. 010 Publishers.

Smith, D. W. (2008). Phenomenology. In E. N. Zalta (Ed.), *Stanford Encyclopedia of Philosophy*. The Metaphysics Research Lab.

Tabb, P. J., & Senem Deviren, A. (2014). The greening of architecture: A critical history and survey of contemporary sustainable architecture and urban design. Ashgate Publishing Limited.

Umberto, E. (1997). Function and Sign: The Semiotics of Architecture. In *Rethinking Architecture* (pp. 173-186). Routledge.

Van Der Ryn, S., & Cowan, S. (2007). *Ecological Design, 10th Anniversary Edition*. Island Press.

William McDonough Architects. (1992). *The Hannover Principles: Design for Sustainability*. Paper presented at the EXPO 2000, The World's Fair, Hannover, Germany.

Wines, J. (2000). *Green Architecture*. Taschen.

CHAPTER 3

EDITORS' PREFACE

While Cucuzzella proposes that being sustainable architecture is a complex ontological reality, Nada Tarkhan highlights that what is perceived as sustainable today might be a result of market dynamics such as technology push and market demand. She focuses on the case of wellness in buildings, its standards and norms, its technologies and its data using a case study in a commercial office building. The essay puts in question whether the current wellness-heavy sustainable architecture discourse has emerged from an ideological foundation or market-drivers. While no one can question the importance of human wellness in the larger scope of sustainable architecture, we should question the financial drivers that shape and reinforce the standardized technical discourse on the topic. She highlights how architects are now expected to present and engage in this new form of technical wellness discourse – a process that implicitly discredits the discipline's centuries-long tradition of attending to the quality of space as fundamental to human wellbeing. We arrive at a complex vicious cycle: where market demand for improvements in efficiency is answered through measurement technologies (sensors and others), which provide new data that continuously reshape the discourse of sustainable architecture, before increasing the market demand, requiring more data-driven efficiency and setting the cycle again. In this cycle, the qualitative dimensions of the architecture are marginalized to make increasingly more space for the techno-scientific figures and presentations.

Technological trajectories: Assessing the role of sensing in design

Nada Tarkhan
Massachusetts Institute of Technology (MIT)

INTRODUCTION

The paths to innovation in the built environment have been evolving to cater to ever-increasing data flow access. Architectural narratives have expanded to adopt methods of assessments, measurement and calibration that attempt to decipher received information and use it to inform design decisions. With this expansion, we have witnessed a simultaneous rise in design awareness and a deeper questioning of the commodification of data as it pertains to new architectural modalities. The phrase *Technological trajectories* can be defined as the paths by which innovation occurs. The emergence of the above advancements is the product of the interplay between scientific progression, economic factors and institutional variables (Dosi, 1981). A significant part of understanding technological advancements in architecture involves assessing their persistence and their contributions to defining the sustainable design discourse. Both technological paradigms' adoptions and the determinants that precede them are equally important to analyze when assessing the power of technological adoption. In the built environment, technological manifestation has influenced many aspects of design—from building automation across various systems (electrical, mechanical, etc.) to advanced Indoor Environmental Quality (IEQ) sensing and monitoring. A mathematical scalar analysis may help us delve into this topic further and understand its magnitude of importance and implications for the field of sustainable design.

In mathematics, scale analysis of a complex equation helps identify both the parameters that are key to solving the equation and the ones that are of less importance. In this context, it is perhaps worthy to use this as an analogy through which to view technological advancements: those that can be used to define the sustainable design discourse and those that exist to aid an operation. While outcomes outside of this binary are possible, the characterization is an attempt to dissect the discourse and reflect on the contributions of several emerging innovations. This dissection becomes particularly relevant when looking at the information that can be obtained from different sensing technologies and their

Technological trajectories

respective design implications throughout time. In an effort to mimic the scale analysis process, this chapter will evaluate the impact of both the technological and technogenic through a scalar analysis of its own. The technological defines the process, whereas the technogenic refers to its product. The scalar analysis process starts with identifying the parameters and variables of the equation (system boundaries) and their relative magnitude as well as their respective spheres of influence thus far. This will be carried out through a brief history of architectural sensing systems and an evaluation of their relative impacts and codependences. Secondly, the chapter will attempt to assess the sensing systems' magnitude and the role they play in defining sustainability and wellness discourse. This step will be carried out through an examination of case studies concerning both building assessments and emerging certifications. This is where the order of magnitude and influence is assessed. At this level of scalar analysis, the sub-scales, consisting of physical, temporal and digital elements are explored in greater depth. Finally, in analyzing these sub-scales, we establish an understanding of the dependencies, reflect on their persistence and establish an understanding of the modes under which these technological trajectories operate.

Figure 3.1 Scalar analysis

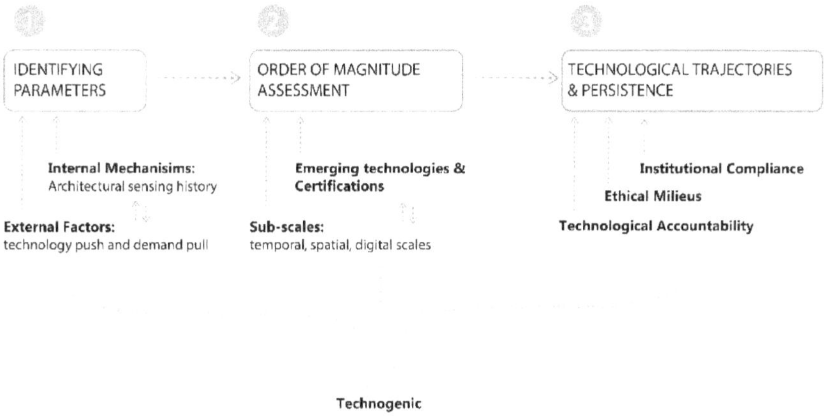

IDENTIFYING PARAMETERS	ORDER OF MAGNITUDE ASSESSMENT	TECHNOLOGICAL TRAJECTORIES & PERSISTENCE
Internal Mechanisims: Architectural sensing history	**Emerging technologies & Certifications**	**Institutional Compliance**
		Ethical Milieus
External Factors: technology push and demand pull	**Sub-scales:** temporal, spatial, digital scales	**Technological Accountability**

Technogenic

An imperative step in numerical problem solving is the simplification process: reducing the number of variables to streamline the solving process. In this case, however, the intention is to simplify such that the solution becomes one that has an extrapolated trajectory towards a critical technological assimilation. Such a process would give us a solution space capable of providing a more malleable framework instead of an absolute resolution. It is important to note that, while this analysis process follows a more standardized approach, it identifies a broader ontological outlook on the field that makes the overall mathematical parallel still quite impressionistic. It must also be established that an intuitive approach to design must not be forgone or traded off for a more prescriptive one where social, economic and contextual factors are disregarded

Moreover, the chapter will explore not only how contemporary innovation streams can be identified, but also how their role in shaping the sustainable design discourse can be assessed. The sustainability agenda has itself seen many assimilations over the past 20 years. In what has been most predominant, both the mechanistic and the qualitative must be combined to give rise to an architecture that is more comprehensive and inclusive of concerns. In what follows, we examine emerging narratives, methods and techniques that have been central to the idea of sensing and response in architecture. Both the modes by which these terminologies have been defined and their sphere of utilization will be examined. The chapter will attempt to discuss in depth the preconditions that allow technology to become an enabler for design and when technology becomes a consequential output. A roadmap of this analysis is summarized in Figure 3.1.

A HISTORY OF TECHNOLOGICAL RESPONSE

In Dosi's historical analysis of technological progression (1982), he states that "Theories of technical change have generally been classified into two broad categories: namely demand-pull and technology-push". His writings indicate that the ambiguities of demand-pull theories are not sufficient indicators that market demand alone is a mover of innovative activity. A technological-push track to innovation, on the other hand, relies on advancements themselves to predict the direction of technical change. This, however, becomes equally challenging as progression is seldom linear, and the uncertainty associated with technological advancement and invention is usually high. It also fails to capture the complex nature of feedback loops between the user, economy and technology. While emerging primarily from economic theory, Dosi's analogies shed light on the complexities of technological adoption and set the stage for analysis to proceed. Moreover, identifying the external influences and internal discourse mechanisms behind various technological adoptions helps in evaluating the system boundaries needed for the scalar analysis to proceed. In addition to carrying out a scalar analysis, we will look to see where technology has been a reactive mechanism (demand-driven) and the variation between instances where it has formed a more interactive relationship with other fields (a combination of demand-pull and technology-push). These concepts reiterate the idea that different modes of advancements are governed by different non-linear drivers that are continuously evolving.

The notion of architectural response has allowed us to interface with our surroundings in a number of unprecedented ways. Surely, passive techniques in global vernacular typologies have exhibited climatic response and established a deeper contextual dialogue than some of the construction we see today. This has very much been driven by a demand to create shelter while coexisting with environmental conditions. Beyond vernacular parallels, the response intended here is that which enables us to understand and quantify human behaviour, occupant patterns and systems use through the aid of instrumentation that collects data from our environments. As these sensory technologies unravel before us, we must be wary of their use, intention and magnitude of impact. To echo what has been stated previously, understanding the persistence of these technologies is key to reverse-engineering their impact. Andrzej Zarzycki (2018) argues that "The knowledge embedded in the developments of analog sensors and actuators is transferable to other disciplines, however, it awaits meaningful architectural responses and applications".

The intentions behind environmental responses are varied and could represent different building typologies, design stages and system designs. Furthermore, spatial inquiry, performance validation and design iteration are just a few examples of guiding motives for studying buildings' capacity to respond to differing conditions. In the context of building sensing, environmental response pertains to the outcome or action that is desired and the building level at which technological automation is integrated. For instance, on a macro level, there may be an external shading structure that responds to sun angles to optimize daylight access to the interior space across the seasons. At a smaller scale, a sensor that measures CO_2 concentration in the air and adjusts a mechanical system operation may be considered.

In an effort to encompass the full spectrum of intentions, we must broaden the boundaries of the sustainability field. It is important to note that, like solving any mathematical problem, we can choose to do this in isolation, or we can draw helpful external parameters. In reality, models of research and practice are seldom closed equations that are only solved by the aid of internal parameters. A more realistic analogy would acknowledge the co-dependency exhibited in an open system of response. For instance, it is impossible to assess indoor air quality without reference to an outside concentration measurement. Thus, external conditions and influences are key to setting up an analytical framework. Similarly, an isolated approach to the field would consider only the numerical components of sensing technologies and energy performance analysis "while ignoring the idea that architecture, as a synthesis of civil processes, is an expression of constructive techniques and typological transformations developed throughout history" (Scardigno, 2014).

The definite potential that technology holds stems from its purpose and mode of conduct (Hensel, 2017). Key operational motives have varied throughout history and evolved to prioritize different goals. The conversation on energy efficiency is central to the origins of automation and sensing in buildings. With the depletion of resources and global climatic changes, the energy and technological innovation's interdependence has become quite clear —where technology, in this instance, has been a reaction to a growing need and consciousness. Many buildings we see today are integrated with a sophisticated network of sensors meant to improve occupant comfort and energy-efficient operations to achieve the desired level of building response. We have witnessed significant advancements in the field of centralized building operation—such as using Building Management Systems (BMS) to provide fault diagnostics, connected light, HVAC meters and occupancy sensors. The existence of this multi-parallel interfacing means that systems can be programmed to follow a performance schedule and detect when users are occupying a space, only spending energy when that space is being used or occupied. All of this is made possible by an array of passive infrared sensors (PIRs) as well as photocells that pick up on light and CO_2, humidity and temperature levels. Through a set of controls, the systems adjust their internal parameters (such as ventilation rates, coil temperatures and luminaire intensities) to respond to a set of pre-defined spatial performance ranges.

The speed of technological advancement, lower cost, increased liability and the growing need for data have all hastened the adoption of sensory technologies in buildings. Beyond sensing, advancements in high-performance façade design (such as windows with higher thermal performance) have enabled the construction of buildings with narrower floorplates, such that occupants can inhabit the perimeter spaces and have access to light, ventilation and views (Choi et al., 2012). Here, we see that design decisions share an interdependence with the direction in which technology has advanced. In some cases, however, the relationship between technology and design is more complex and represents a more inherently unpredictable association. We cannot predict an exact technological adoption scenario across all types of building-integrated gadgets, but efforts to understand codependences across the transdisciplinary nature of the field of building automation are beginning to take shape.

Data & Emergent modalities

Coupled building-sensing frameworks are increasing in both complexity and held potential —potential related not only to the acquisition of data, but to the fidelity and reliability of its assessment in design, as well. While uncertainty still dominates the direction of adoption, the presence of high-resolution monitoring and advancements in large-scale silicon processing have catapulted design and building science into a new era of data management. The building profession must account for dynamic spatial adaptation, material and system lifecycles and a myriad of other shifting usages. Ultimately, developments surrounding big data have allowed us to anticipate how buildings will be used and to prepare better for the future (Linder et al., 2017). Massive computing power and access to real-time data have not only refined the accuracy of the information we obtain, but also the speed in which it becomes accessible to us. Feedback mechanisms are powered by ubiquitous sensing equipment that now has the capacity to form statistical correlations, exemplifying advancements in the world of machine learning and artificial intelligence.

Smart thermostats are a good example of advanced building sensing, having the capacity to program themselves to occupant patterns and automatically switch on and off various building operations. The thermostats detect information on occupancy and use it to adjust lighting levels and ventilation airflows to cater to the exact number of occupants in a space. Furthermore, they store this statistical information and use it to develop long term seasonal operations without any manual user input. The output is an optimized condition balancing idealized system functionality catered to users' needs. In the data science world, this is what is referred to as a *data-driven system*, as opposed to a conventional *knowledge-based* one (Dubois et al., 2000). In essence, the intent of a machine learning approach is to handle a multitude of variables in instances where predicting an outcome is difficult. This contrasts with a rule-based system, which handles just a few variables, and follows a more prescriptive model for operations. A knowledge-based system gives us the capacity to solve complex problems and provides data that we can use to learn and adapt our spaces. We receive answers to questions we did not ask, which can be quite powerful in providing insight into how spaces perform. This is fundamental to many emerging technologies that intend to evolve the way we use energy in our buildings.

As highlighted above, the development of advanced technologies and market have driven demand in the built environment to have a prominent role in defining usage patterns. Advancements surrounding more pervasive building networks, sensor-frameworks and computational power, have aided functionalities such as energy tracking. The codependence between market forces and the emergence of technologies is evident in trends in both BMS system development and the approaches taken to sub-meter and track individualized building usage components such as fresh air, chilled water and hot water for mechanical system usage. Tracking these items has no doubt provided unprecedented insight and has given us more control over the desired level of building response we wish to achieve. It is quite consequential then, that these same parameters become an important part of tracking sustainability metrics and enhancing overall building performance and resource efficiency.

In recent years, however, sustainability discourse has expanded beyond energy management to encompass occupant comfort and wellness. Our ubiquity of sophisticated models and analytical techniques must now address a wider set of concerns and design considerations. A market—or demand-pull backed up by scientific grounding—is evident in this case. The opportunities and challenges of emerging technological frameworks are now to be evaluated against a new set of metrics. The challenge that the next generation of tools must address is the quantification of wellness concepts and indicators that operate outside the realm of traditional building operational measurements and whose basis is rapidly evolving. The implications of this will be highlighted in the following sections through the identification of emerging metrics and by addressing the various developed wellness vocabularies.

FRAMING STANDARDS: IDENTIFYING THE WELLNESS NEXUS

The focus on health and wellbeing in buildings has gained a great deal of attention in recent years. Americans, on average, spend approximately 90% of their time indoors (US EPA, 1989). A study carried out by Gallup on the American Workplace identified that approximately 67% of employees in 2016 were disengaged at work. While the reasons were varied, the interior environment has been identified as one of the main contributing factors. In addition to this, there has been strong scientific interest in researching and identifying direct correlations between interior environment and occupant health. Noise, light, temperature and air quality have all been proven to impact occupant well-being and, in more extreme cases, have caused health issues such as respiratory problems. In this light, failure to account for the physiological effects of building design is no longer acceptable, and energy conservation cannot be held up as the sole goal of building sustainability. In what many have described as the new *green*, wellness has come to play a central role in identifying better ways of both understanding and assessing the performance of our buildings.

From the demise of singular-goal-focused resource efficiency to the increased awareness of occupant health, the built environment has been evolving to alter its current sustainability purview and design priority list. With the rise of certifications such as the WELL Building Standard[1], architects and engineers have come face to face with new assessment metrics that span materials, air quality and temperature, as well as space planning and ergonomics. The WELL Building Standard puts the occupant at the center of design and includes a more comprehensive list of building strategies that fall into seven categories: Nourishment, Light, Air, Movement, Water, Comfort and Mind. To this end, assessment frameworks and design strategies have to be developed to address the new generation of building certifications and occupant needs. While the industry has grown accustomed to green certification standards such as LEED[2] and BREEAM[3], the road map to navigating wellness is still in development and has not yet been fully incorporated in practice. While some measurements and metrics remain timid, the financial grounding of expenditure on employees is significant enough to develop a solid

---

[1] Standard launched in 2014. For more information: https://www.wellcertified.com/
[2] Leadership in Energy and Environmental Design. For more information: https://new.usgbc.org/leed
[3] Building Research Establishment Environmental Assessment Method. For more information: https://www.breeam.com/

business case. Economic analysis has shown that about 90% of business operating costs are staff costs in salaries and benefits (WGBC, 2014). This means that a 2% increase in employee productivity through increased performance could result in roughly $6/SF while a 2% decrease in energy use could yield savings of $0.06/SF (JLL, 2014). Workplace environments have become the prime candidate for these studies since they are where people spend most of their day and where productivity and cognitive performance can be best investigated (Heschong Mahone Group Inc., 2003). Employers are growing increasingly interested in ways of both reducing health spending and absenteeism and enhancing productivity. Certification aside, buildings should strive to improve their environmental conditions and utilize state of the art technological practices to address the research revelations of contemporary sustainability discourse. It is often the case, however, that pervasive market adoption only occurs when strategies become formalized in building certification requirements. This is particularly evident in the case of interior materials. Material ingredients in paints, specifically, are a good example of this. Research showing that VOC's (Volatile Organic Compounds) cause a number of health issues drive the market to demand low VOC paint products (Wallace, 1993). Resultingly, then, advancements in manufacturing and product knowledge allow paints to be manufactured with lower levels of toxins and volatile organic compounds (VOCs), despite their having previously been considered integral to the performance of paint. Following this, certifications and declare labels emerge to guarantee material performance and become integrated in building certifications—such as the material disclosure credits under LEED. The demand for material transparency and the technology to achieve it go hand in hand in this case and embody the push-pull effect identified earlier in this chapter. In addition to this, there is a temporal effect occurring, where cycles such as the one explained above, refine themselves and shape the sustainability discourse through time. An illustration of this cycle is presented in Figure 3.2.

With regards to other areas of comfort and wellness surrounding air quality, temperature and light, design is no longer expected to cater to a statistical average, but to individuals with varying needs and preferences (Andrzej, 2018). Studies have shown that altering internal space parameters can influence cognitive performance (World Green Building Council, 2014). Identifying positively contributing factors to health is key to developing wellness strategies in building design. A study carried out by the Harvard T.H. Chan School of Public Health set up a framework to understand the cognitive impacts of working in a green-certified building versus a non-certified building (Allen et al., 2015). Green buildings were identified in five U.S. cities as those surpassing ASHRAE[4] Standard 62.1 for ventilation requirements (ASHRAE, 2019) as well as having LEED Green

---

[4] American Society of Heating, Refrigerating and Air-Conditioning Engineers. For more information: https://www.ashrae.org/about

Building Certification and low total VOC concentrations. The study found that, on average, participants in high-performance buildings scored 26.4% higher on cognitive tests than those in non-certified ones. The cognitive functioning domains included; crisis response, task orientation, information seeking, information usage, strategy as well as basic and applied activity levels. While the subjects were aware that they were participating in a study, they were not told the three testing parameters of; outdoor fresh air intake, CO_2 levels and VOCs (Allen et at., 2015).

Figure 3.2 Cycle of innovation and market adoption in the wellness field

① Scientific research- advancments in science propel the market to demand better products

② Advancements in manufacturing- technological advancement to cater to new scientific discoveries

③ Emergence of labels- industry standards to guarantee product quality and diffrentiate it in the market

④ Formalization in building Certifications & Codes- backed by scientific research and market demand

In the field of lighting design, research has been focusing on tunable lighting that changes colour temperature throughout the day. While visual sensations of light and the anthropology of luminosity have been studied at length, emerging research has indicated that the quality of light we get exposed to throughout the day influences our internal clock and sleep-wake cycle. This is what is referred to as the circadian rhythm, or biological cycle that occurs every 24 hours. Different light levels and colour temperatures can suppress and control the release of melatonin at night (Webb, 2006) and in turn enhance alertness during daytime hours. Given this, lighting fixtures must now consider both spectral output and artificial radiation, as well as tunable controls and sensors to account appropriately for human physiological effects.

Internet of Things (IoT) methods, coupled with user-feedback centred IEQ assessments, enable architects to develop a more intimate understanding of building occupant patterns and behaviours. IoT can be described as a "network of dedicated physical objects (things) that contain embedded technology to communicate and sense or interact with their internal states or the external environment" (Hung, 2017). IoT methods have revolutionized data analytics and provided immense connectivity potentials in building systems. It is these sensing capabilities that allow us to better understand our interior environments and their impact on occupants. According to Gartner (Hung, 2017), by the end of 2020, more than 65% of enterprises (up from 30% in 2017) will adopt IoT products. In the next section, a case study in an office environment will use an IoT platform to study various internal parameters. The focus will be on understanding performance and health implications as well as identifying the technologies used to conduct the study.

Moving forward with our scalar analysis, we look to evaluate the respective sphere of influence and the role that emerging technological frameworks have played in the wellness discourse. We see that digital sensor technology is ultimately a key participant in how the wellness discourse is being validated and defined. Numeric sensor-based research and foresight enable building scientists to convince owners, architects and others involved in building design to adopt wellness practices. Here, we see an intricate relationship that exists between scientific advancement, economic backing and stakeholder interest and motivation. For corresponding design criteria to exist, the digital infrastructure had to exist to support its manifestation and pervasive use in a building standard. Without scientific backing or economical grounds, there is little tractive potential for the adoption of wellness strategies in the field. On both the temporal and the digital scale, these advancements have been shown to evolve themselves over time and influence the development of the wellness agenda.

Designing the Feedback loop: Post Occupancy Evaluation

We have identified that the technological feedback loop provides an integral outlook into performance and has shown to influence the field of high-performance design. Rubin and Elder (1980) argue that instrumented research plays a key role in the development of standards. Setting up an effective sensing and analysis framework for Post Occupancy Evaluation (POE) is key to obtaining results that have the potential to provide reliable performance insight and design feedback. The physical (spatial) sub-scale is crucial to the application of advanced digital infrastructures, where sensors are used to help us better understand how our spaces function. Post Occupancy Evaluation has been used widely in the building industry to assess ambient conditions' performance in buildings and their effect on occupants. It can be defined as the "the process of evaluating buildings in a systematic and rigorous manner after they have been built and occupied for some time" (Preiser et al., 1988).

Research incorporating field measurements and feedback from occupants has shown that there is a divide between design intent and actual building performance (Loftness et al., 2009). While this divide may be the product of anything from occupant behaviour to system degradation over time, sensing frameworks must be set up to ask the right questions and address the root causes of performance issues.

In a case study focused on the development of sensing infrastructure, the Arup Boston office set out to carry a Post Occupancy study to compare its old and new office spaces. The new office was designed with wellness strategies in mind and has been awarded LEED Platinum, WELL Gold and Fitwel[5] 3-star certification. The study utilized an in-house designed sensor kit (shown in Figure 3.3) that recorded environmental parameters including dry bulb temperature (C), relative humidity (%), horizontal illumination level (lux), carbon dioxide (CO_2) concentration (ppm), particulate matter (PM 1, 2.5,10) and VOCs (Volatile Organic Compounds). The study's three primary goals were agility, data accuracy and the processing of large quantities of data.

Figure 3.3 Sensor kit for indoor environmental parameters

Notes:
- © Arup

The research was designed to carry out a comparative analysis between the different offices and space types (kitchen, workspace, meeting room) within each office. As such, fine-tuned system anomaly detection and diagnostics were not explored. This would have required a different suite of sensing tools integrated with the offices' ventilation systems. Another significant goal of the study was to understand the connections between various building strategies and employee satisfaction. As such, a questionnaire, which was modelled after the BUS (Building Use Studies) survey[6], was distributed to the employees that The survey asked

---

[5] For emore information: https://fitwel.org/
[6] For more information: https://www.busmethodology.org.uk/

Technological trajectories

employees to rate their satisfaction with their office's environmental quality as well as other aspects of mental comfort across a seven-point scale of satisfaction (Very unsatisfied, moderately unsatisfied, slightly unsatisfied, neutral, slightly satisfied, moderately satisfied, very satisfied).

At the Core of Arup's study was the development of an IoT Web tool that displayed sensor readings in real-time. The intention was to utilize state of the art equipment and software to streamline data parsing and access sequences as well as enable instantaneous visualization (Tarkhan, 2018). A custom script was written to log and load the data at one-minute intervals. The data feed connected to the internal Arup network, making it accessible to all employees across all of the company's offices. There are currently four other offices within Arup that have the same sensor kit, making cross-office comparison possible through a single digital platform. The algorithm was meant to enhance the data analytic capability of off-the-shelf sensor products while providing an inexpensive solution to mass-utilization. The display page of the dashboard is shown in Figure 3.4.

Figure 3.4 Preview of the online web-tool's dashboard

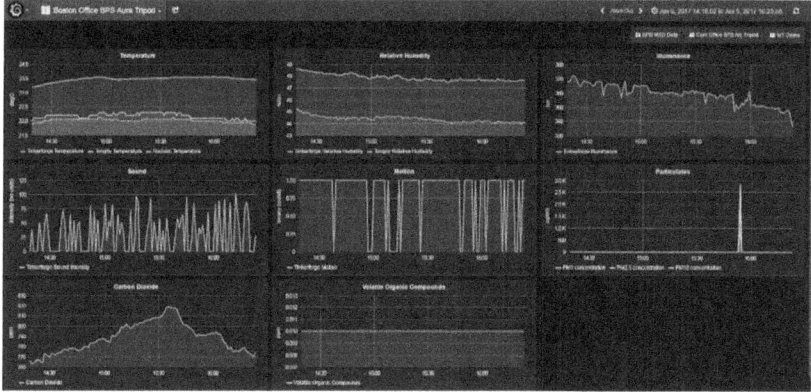

Notes:
- Showing (from left to right): Row 1: temperature, relative humidity and, illuminance; Row 2: sound, motion and particulates; Row 3: carbon dioxide and volatile organic compounds
- © Arup

To aid the reader in understanding the data obtained from this analysis, an excerpt from the results is shown in Figure 3.5. The CO_2 and light levels were monitored for a period of three consecutive days in each location of the office. A total of five locations were analyzed: the kitchen space, a meeting room and three work areas. The results display both the quantitative sensor readings and the survey results.

Air Quality

The CO_2 sensor readings plotted in Figure 3.5 show the old office and new office readings alongside each other. The statistical variations during occupied work hours (8 am to 6 pm) were plotted. According to the Illinois Department of Public Health, the recommended average CO_2 concentration for indoor environments is 800ppm. Levels above 1,000 ppm are likely to lead to detrimental health effects. The results show that CO2 levels generally stayed below 800ppm. On average, higher CO_2 levels were recorded in the new office than in the old office. There were three plausible explanations for this difference. The absence of an outside air economizer in the new building limited fresh air intake, leading to a slower flush-out of CO_2. In addition to this, the new office witnessed a reduction of about 20% in workstation area per employee, meaning that occupancy density increased. Finally, another contributing factor was façade infiltration. The old office had a less air-tight façade that allowed more air to come in through window joints.

Figure 3.5 CO_2 measurements in old and new office for one working day

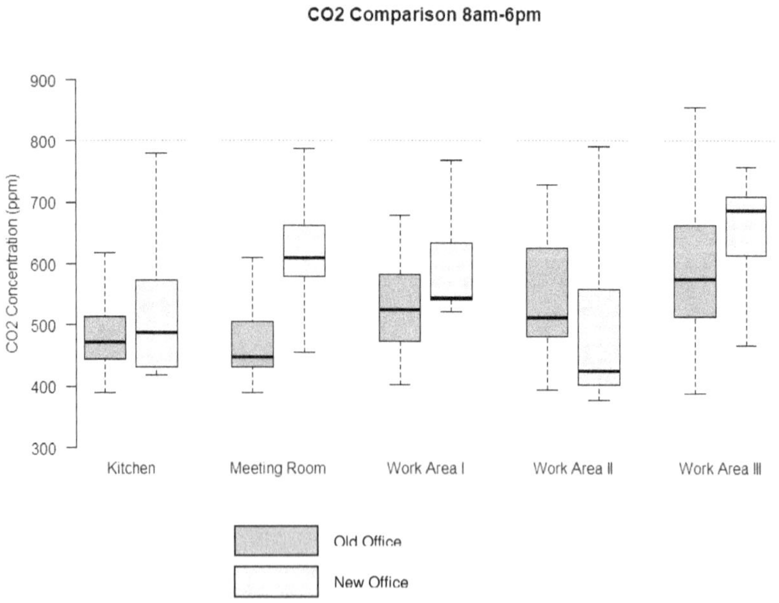

Notes:

- © Arup

Despite the correlations exhibited in these measurements, the reported survey results show that 72% of staff said they were satisfied with the air quality, as compared to 13% in the old office. The discrepancy between measured results and survey responses brings up a number of interesting questions concerning occupant perception. Possible explanations include the psychological perception of a new office space and the fact that measurements did not exceed the maximum threshold of 1000ppm (and hence differences may not have been overly noticeable).

Light

The lighting measurements indicated a significant improvement from the old office to the new. The new office had been designed with a circadian tunable lighting system that changed color temperature throughout the day to align with the sun and astronomical time-clock (seen in Figure 3.6). The daily operation can be seen in Figure 6. To capture the lighting levels and spectrum data, a new metric was used, referred to as EML (Equivalent Melanopic Lux). The recommended levels under the WELL Building standard are 200 EML for 75% of workstations. The results of the in-situ measurements showed that 75% of the new office workstations meet this requirement, as opposed to 54% in the old office (seen in Figure 3.7). Measurements were all taken between 9 am and 1 pm and showed that some workstations extending deeper in the floor plate do not meet the light level requirement prescribed. With reference to reported occupant satisfaction levels, 75% of employees reported that the lighting environment was comfortable, compared to 42% in the old office. Another important factor to consider when analyzing lighting in the space is glare, which can be caused by too much daylighting and contrast in the scene. 81% percent of staff reported a satisfaction with glare levels at workstations in the new office as opposed to 51% in the old office.

Figure 3.6 Daily circadian lighting operation

Mid-day
Color temperature
set at 5000K

Evening
Color temperature
set at 3000K

Notes:

- © Arup

Figure 3.7 Lighting equivalent melanopic lux (EML) measurements for one working day

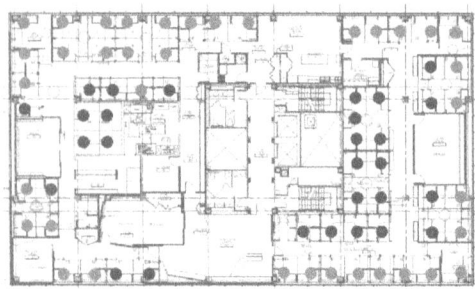

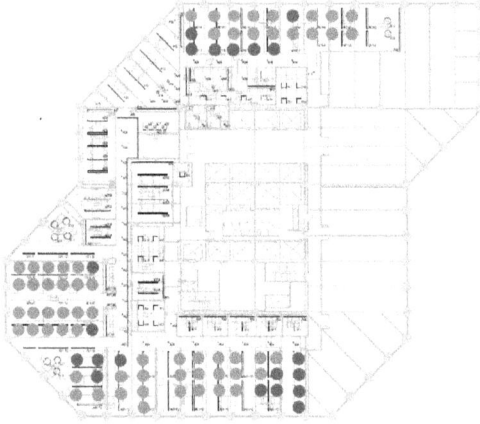

Notes:
- © Arup
- (top) old office, (bottom) new office

Evaluating the Sensing Framework

As discussed in the previous section, Arup's sensing technology enabled an understanding of the physical performance of its offices. In addition to this, the spatial monitoring process aided the award of the WELL certification. A key step to certifying a project is Performance Verification,[7] which involves WELL Assessors visiting an office space and taking in-situ measurements to validate compliance with recommended standards, such as the ASHRAE 55 for comfort (ASHRAE, 2017). This process covers a set of environmental parameters similar to those recorded by the sensor kit. Having carried out the analysis in advance,

---

[7] For more information: https://www.wellcertified.com/en/articles/get-know-well-what-performance-verification

the Arup Boston office was able to adjust design variables (where possible) and incorporate feedback to ensure compliance with the required thresholds and come closer to addressing occupant comfort. Here, the implication on design becomes more direct, as it provides an avenue for feedback that would not typically be available in traditional design and construction workflows.

To expand on the above, we must differentiate between design feedback and a design method. The latter embodies a process, while the former defines a useful mechanism for evaluating implemented strategies. This is quite imperative both to the scalar analysis at hand and to identifying contributions to the sustainable discourse and magnitude of influence on design. In another study, focused on POE analysis of twenty Federal Buildings, the authors note that work environments today "must anticipate high levels of spatial and technological change by providing responsive thermal and air quality delivery systems" (Choi et al., 2012). The gradual responsive updating of buildings' systems over time enables spatial adaptability and a higher degree of occupant satisfaction. In the light of this required adaptation, sensors must continue to monitor and provide feedback to aid design evolution over time. As such, methods of data collection must advance themselves to keep up with increasing speeds of information processing and user interfacing.

Another important factor when embarking on studies like the above is the degree of scientific methodology and rigor applied. There are a multitude of variables involved in this, including setting the appropriate sampling schemes and formulating precise questions, as well as coordinating the experimental set up and data flows. The accuracy of data obtained is highly dependent on the refinement of the sensing process by which measurements are obtained. It is also important to note that experimentational and methodological frameworks are not one-size-fits-all in nature. In the case of the Arup Boston office, Post-Occupancy Evaluation and high-level analysis were carried out to understand the IEQ differences and the general employee perceptions. If the analysis was more concerned with envelope performance or system operations, we would need to deploy a multitude of sensors that would be mounted at different heights and locations. The monitoring period would also have to be elongated to capture seasonal and diurnal operations. In short, the digital, temporal and spatial scales would all need to be adjusted to address a different set of inquiries.

On the potential of scalability, we find that various POE studies have moved away from encompassing just singular buildings to now span entire portfolios or databases of buildings. In this context, drawing conclusions and parallels must be carried out with caution as standardizing conditions becomes a bigger challenge. For instance, when drawing conclusions on a larger set of buildings under a portfolio, differences in building functions, systems installed, construction and fuel usage may make comparisons more difficult. The data obtained from an office building cannot be compared to a residential building, as occupancy and a whole set of design attributes would differ. In summary, data obtained across a portfolio of buildings must incorporate methodological processes to account for this and draw sound, comparable results. These tensions, between local (micro) data and portfolio (macro) data, can be mediated by technological normalization techniques such as grouping and sampling data based on similarities in design, or using by statistical analysis to identify outliers. Ultimately, the importance of proper analysis methods becomes magnified in the case of larger portfolio projects.

THE TECHNOGENIC

Having identified the factors and determinants driving the relationship between technology and present-day ecological ideologies that define the field of sustainable design, we now reach a point of discourse convergence. This convergence introduces the final step of the scalar analysis, which looks at a product or solution (the technogenic) and reflects on the orders of magnitude discussed. Fundamentally, the technogenic can be seen as a by-product of every step of the scalar analysis, where there is technologic output presented. The persistence of the technogenic, however, is defined under the interplay of three main orders: technological accountability and preoccupations, ethical milieus, and institutional compliance.

Technological Accountability and Preoccupations

Perhaps one of the most discussed topics surrounding sustainability and the power of technology is accountability. The process of upgrading data to information can follow many paths, including ones in which interrogating this data must lead to actionable results (Hensel, 2017). The outcomes we yield from these processes are not always free of fault or discrepancy, and we must be mindful of the approaches we take to data management. Concise frameworks must be set in a place where fault detection becomes entangled in the technological terrain.

Given this, we must be wary of the technogenic, or the possible outcomes of a discipline that relies excessively on emerging technological paradigms. Aiding an operation under scalar analysis (as highlighted previously in this Chapter) is shown in the narrative and case studies discussed where operational data has contributed to the enhancement of wellness, sensor-detection of building performance anomalies and overall enhancement of interior environments. The level of detail in the data measured by these technologies is rapidly evolving and providing us with new avenues of possibility. If such assessment methods become the definition of wellness on the other hand, it can shift the discourse in more obstinate directions. Having advanced sensing networks in place does not guarantee data accuracy or well-placed motives that intend to push the field forward. Similarly, having the right intentions and the wrong framework does not lead to progressive results. Hensel warns of this in his writings on "Loci of Disruptiveness", as he reflects on the "*Technocene* [emphasis added]". He states that contemporary use of technology in architecture is dominated by products developed for spectacle rather than for public good. Developing institutional codes is thus key to moderating these industry and technological emergence relationships and ensuring scientists, engineers, architects and building owners ultimately comply with the standards set in place.

What we have seen in some more convoluted histories is a preoccupation with certain modes of technogenic outcomes. In his writings on the history of energetics and insulation, Moe (2014) outlines a pre-occupation for using with R-values[8] and insulation to achieve energy efficiency in building design. Insulation, he states, does not mediate between the building and its surroundings but rather isolates it from external opportunities and integration. He traces the scientific advancements he identifies to refrigeration and the persistence of a narrative that has dominated building thermal envelope design even though internal environments seldom operate in steady-state conditions (which is the case for refrigeration applications). The transfer of technology from thermal theory developed for refrigeration to buildings, in this example, fails to acknowledge the physiological needs of buildings and the nature of their transient internal environments. What we learn from this precedent is that technology that is borrowed or repurposed may result in a short-sighted adaptation or a less than ideal outcome. We are not immune to mismatched persistence and applications when we speak of sensor technology and its integration in our design solutions. We must be wary of over-reliability on sensing and building automation.

Ethical Milieus

Another issue to consider is the progression of responsive sensor networks and their use beyond the field of environmental design. A better understanding of scientific methodologies and frameworks that ensure that occupant-based research is conducted scientifically and ethically is imperative. Data acquisition has become commonplace in many fields and industries and has opened a myriad of ethical and data-culture questions. In this chapter, we have discussed and reflected on sensors and sensor-driven responses that are specific to indoor environmental quality. There are numerous other sensor types that perform

---

[8] R-value is a measure of how well a 3D barrier can resist conductive heat flow

other tasks such as tracking occupancy and space utilization. In addition to this, wearable sensor technology exposes users to unprecedented threats involving unlawful data acquisition and privacy. The implications of advanced building monitoring techniques and hyper-connectedness must be managed appropriately. Big data has the capacity to aid formulating new design methods and feedback avenues, but the critical question is that of who will be given the opportunity to benefit from the data collected. Surrounding ethical concerns too give rise to questions such as *How must we then navigate through this technological frontier?* and *how must data be de-limited or controlled?*

Some strategies that have been employed include using fully encrypted data processing platforms, using fully tested, secure and reliable sensors and being transparent about what data will eventually be used for (Hensel, 2017). While these strategies help mediate privacy issues, they are not entirely free of concern. Individual data points may be protected from third-party access, but aggregated findings can be open to the public. To counter this, data governance laws have expanded to adopt clauses where the user has the right to restrict or object to the use of their data in certain studies. In addition to this, users have come to be viewed as data holders whose data third party analysis services are only able to process and then release. The risks that future technologies must focus on are that of privacy protection in cloud computing, where data is stored in multiple network locations.

Institutional Compliance

Technological empowerment cannot exist outside an analysis of institutional drivers. The demand pull and technology push are surface-level characterizations of a much more complex system. Design and legislative institutions exercise control over the built environment, and their mandates take the form of building codes, standards and certifications that reflect market constraints and stakeholder objectives. The ultimate goal is advancing the sustainability field.

Moreover, following a checklist approach to design raises fundamental ontological questions. Should the discipline be defined, advanced and repurposed under the rules and requirements of certifications and standards? It is apparent that the techno-environmental agenda must become more concerned with social, contextual and economic factors in order to be truly sustainable and to survive new paradigms of concern (Lützkendorf & Lorenz, 2006). Sustainable architecture should ultimately strive for social equity, contextual integration and other higher values that can sometimes be difficult to account for in checklists. In accordance with this, the aim of the discipline becomes prescribing a set of design recommendations that can attain a future for diversities across occupants and uses and adapt as needed.

Un-scalable Parameters

It is important to understand the obligations that the various sensing technologies embody. Examining both research and practice-based models provides insight into how technological adoption has occurred in the past and gives us an idea of the direction of contemporary advancements. The methods, technologies, narratives and examples noted in this text are not exhaustive, nor do they encompass all the technological paradigms we witness in the built environment today. Rather, they intend to draw on connections that are under development and that intend to address fluxes of ecological concerns. While some areas of building sustainability have been impacted by technological advancements, it is important to reiterate that the degree of technological adoption should not be tantamount to defining the field.

The persistence of sensing technologies can ultimately be traced back to the persistence of emerging discourses such as wellness, the economic argument for the implementation of emerging sustainability strategies and the readiness of the market to adopt these practices. The deeper interplay of ethical concerns, accountability and institutional mandates governs the willingness of adoption and the integration in design. While these parameters have been identified as orders under a larger scale analysis, constitutively there are other influences that may not be directly scalable. The power of technology to bring about behavioural change is another aspect of automation that deserves an in-depth analysis of its own. In addition to this, the angle of this chapter assesses the technogenic but not the refinement of pedagogical metrics and the need to formulate better questions, which is a challenge that the next generation of technological adoption must cope with to reach higher architectural ideals.

The scalar analysis covered in this chapter has presented a set of parameters that encompass the linkages between systems of technological response, external influences and emerging innovations. On the relative magnitudes of influence in the field of sustainable design, the discussion on energy efficiency, wellness as well as the interplay between the rise of certifications and industry innovations was examined. Here, it was established that there are several subscales that operate between the digital (sensor technology), physical (occupied spaces) and temporal (timeline of development) realms. The final step embodied the solving of this scalar analysis through an evaluation of persistence and the spheres of influence discussed. The concluding persistence of the technological and the technogenic looks at the idealistic refinement of goals, metrics and trajectory of development as it stands. Ultimately, the field of sustainable design is in constant flux and has embodied several emerging concerns that have impacted the way that architecture is practiced and realized. It is evident that design's sphere of concern has expanded to encompass a wider set of phenomena that have both enriched the discourse and opened it up to risks, volatility and promise.

REFERENCES

Allen, J. G., MacNaughton, P., Laurent, J. G. C., Flanigan, S. S., Eitland, E. S., & Spengler, J. D. (2015). Green Buildings and Health. *Current Environmental Health Reports, 2*(3), 250–258. https://doi.org/10.1007/s40572-015-0063-y

ASHRAE. (2017). *ASHRAE/ANSI Standard 55-2017 Thermal environmental conditions for human occupancy.* American Society of Heating, Refrigerating, and Air-Conditioning Engineers.

ASHRAE. (2019). *ANSI/ASHRAE Standard 62.1-2019 Ventilation for Acceptable Indoor Air Quality.* American Society of Heating, Refrigerating and Air-Conditioning Engineers.

Choi, J.-H., Loftness, V., & Aziz, A. (2012). Post-occupancy evaluation of 20 office buildings as basis for future IEQ standards and guidelines. *Energy and Buildings, 46*, 167–175. https://doi.org/10.1016/j.enbuild.2011.08.009

Dosi, G. (1981). *Transmission Mechanisms of Technical Change. Adjustment Problems and Their International Implications.* SERC, University of Sussex.

Dosi, G. (1982). Technological paradigms and technological trajectories. *Research Policy, 11*(3), 147–162. https://doi.org/10.1016/0048-7333(82)90016-6

Dubois, D., Hájek, P., & Prade, H. (2000). Knowledge-Driven versus Data-Driven Logics. *Journal of Logic, Language and Information, 9*(1), 65–89. https://doi.org/10.1023/A:1008370109997

Hensel, M. U. (2017). Loci of Disruptiveness: Reflections on Ethics at the Dawn of the Technocene. *Technology|Architecture + Design, 1*(1), 6–8. https://doi.org/10.1080/24751448.2017.1292786

Heschong Mahone Group Inc. (2003). Windows and Offices: A Study of Office Workers' Performance and the Indoor Environments. California Energy Commission Technical Report.

Hung, M. (Ed.). (2017). *Leading the IoT.* Gartner Inc. https://www.gartner.com/imagesrv/books/iot/iotEbook_digital.pdf

JLL. (2014). Perspectives on Workplace Sustainability. Retrieved from http://www.us.jll.com/united-states/en-us/Documents/Workplace/green-productive-workplace-perspective.pdf

Linder, L., Vionnet, D., Bacher, J.-P., & Hennebert, J. (2017). Big Building Data - a Big Data Platform for Smart Buildings. *Energy Procedia, 122*, 589–594. https://doi.org/10.1016/j.egypro.2017.07.354

Loftness, V., Aziz, A., Choi, J., Kampschroer, K., Powell, K., Atkinson, M., & Heerwagen, J. (2009). The value of post-occupancy evaluation for building occupants and facility managers. *Intelligent Buildings International, 1*(4), 249–268. https://doi.org/10.3763/inbi.2009.SI04/splitsection3

Lützkendorf, T., & Lorenz, D. P. (2006). Using an integrated performance approach in building assessment tools. *Building Research & Information, 34*(4), 334–356. https://doi.org/10.1080/09613210600672914

Moe, K. (2014). *Insulating Modernism Isolated and Non-Isolated Thermodynamics in Architecture.* Birkhäuser Verlag GmbH.

Preiser, W. F. E., Rabinowitz, H. Z., & White, E. T. (1988). *Post-Occupancy Evaluation*. Van Nostrand Reinhold.

Rubin, A. I., & Elder, J. (1980). Building for people behavioral research approaches and directions. U.S. Dept. of Commerce, National Bureau of Standards.

Scardigno, N. (2014). Toward an A Priori Sustainable Architecture. *Arts*, *3*(1), 15–26. https://doi.org/10.3390/arts3010015

Tarkhan, N. (2018). The Development of an Indoor Environmental Monitoring Framework for Post-Occupancy Evaluation using Real-Time Web Tools. *Unpublished manuscript*, IBPSA.

U.S. Environmental Protection Agency (1989). *Report to Congress on indoor air quality*. Volume 2. EPA/400/1-89/001C.

Wallace, L. A. (1993). Response to total exposure assessment methodology (TEAM) study by rosebrook and worm. *Environment International*, *19*(3), 303–306. https://doi.org/10.1016/0160-4120(93)90092-V

Webb, A. R. (2006). Considerations for lighting in the built environment: Non-visual effects of light. *Energy and Buildings*, *38*(7), 721–727. https://doi.org/10.1016/j.enbuild.2006.03.004

World Green Building Council (2014). *Health, Wellbeing & Productivity in Offices*. Retrieved from: www.ukgbc.org/sites/default/files/Health%2520 Wellbeing%2520and%2520Productivity

Zarzycki, A. (2018). Describe, Explain, and Predict. *Technology|Architecture + Design*, *2*(1), 1–1. https://doi.org/10.1080/24751448.2018.1420955

CHAPTER 4

EDITORS' PREFACE

While Tarkhan points to the fact that the techno-scientific measurements and representations marginalize the architectural questions of sustainable building design, Tom Jefferies and Laura Coucill argue that representation of data can in-itself hold a key to advancing sustainable architecture. They start their essay by indicating that while data, might be objective, its representation enforces biases. Specifically, they point to sustainable design data and its human dimensions which in many cases ignore the contingency and context of the data itself, as well as the idiosyncrasies of the people and places it represents. They echo Tarkhan's view that data is a product of choices and technologies and add that it cannot be assumed to be unbiased. Instead of disassociating data from their context and complex networks that make up space and its actors, the essay proposes to explore meaningful and culturally appropriate means of representation which combine quantitative and qualitative dimensions. By exploring different forms of representation relating to sustainability and sustainable architecture, Jefferies and Coucill indicate that while designing based on data has become increasingly common, what they call design-leading approaches, the more appropriate approach would be a design-led approach that does not replace critical thinking by quantitative measures. They highlight that a shift in the representation of sustainable design could result in a change of focus from efficiency-driven metrics towards design for effectiveness. The essay concludes that unquantifiable characteristics could and should be an important dimension of sustainable architecture.

Recognising effectiveness in sustainable design

Tom Jefferies
Queen's University Belfast

Laura Coucill
Manchester School of Architecture

INTRODUCTION

Efficiency in sustainable design is focused on the prevention of calculated and diagnosed risks. It is about achieving measurable, material improvements, without necessarily considering their broader social, spatial, political and environmental risks. Effectiveness is outcome-driven and can require doing things differently or unconventionally. It requires judgement beyond metrics and scales.

Burgeoning quantities of data, which underpin efficiency-driven goals in sustainable design, are becoming increasingly disconnected from the lived experience of space and place. Sustainability exposes this, particularly through differences in how it is captured and represented globally and universally as well as how it manifests itself at local and particular scales. The design of sustainable architecture and infrastructure, therefore, demands re-evaluation with the intention of establishing approaches for achieving effectiveness across a range of scales.

Here, we review the scalar implications of assessing local performance metrics for sustainability with a focus on how efficiency at local, particular scales might not deliver effective sustainable outcomes at broader spatial ones. The work recognises the relationship between space and constructs of society and economics as a significant feature of the way in which spatial scales are demarcated, which, in current, efficiency-driven systems, appears to be disconnected from the metrics which guide the assessment of sustainable space. The result is that efficiency can only apply to clearly defined spatial scales, which are typically, small, limited and controlled (Figure 4.1). The work also explores why growth in data production, capture and processing, that enables the assessment of sustainable space through a greater pool of metrics, may still not necessarily produce sustainable outcomes at

Recognising effectiveness 71

all scales because of the specificity with which data is gathered and the limited frameworks within which it is evaluated.

In the context of sustainability, spatial challenges such as this demand cross-thematic, multi-layered analysis and design approaches that enable the creation of the environmental preconditions to support effective sustainable behaviour and performance across a range of scales. Consideration of spatial dynamics and the complex relationships that transcend spatial boundaries, categories and behaviours are needed in this re-evaluation of sustainable design approaches. This chapter reports on design-led approaches that highlight culturally responsive analysis in contrast to the design-leading outcomes of efficiency-driven methodologies. This type of analysis has been shown to be a starting point for recognising scalar complexity and the social and cultural constructs affecting it. One outcome of a culturally responsive approach might be identifying appropriate conditions for turning latency into opportunity. The first step in this transition requires a conceptual move away from definitions of sustainability that prioritize efficiency to ones that prioritize effectiveness.

Figure 4.1 Visualising the complex relationship between data and space in order to demonstrate the limitations of efficiency-driven approaches to sustainable design

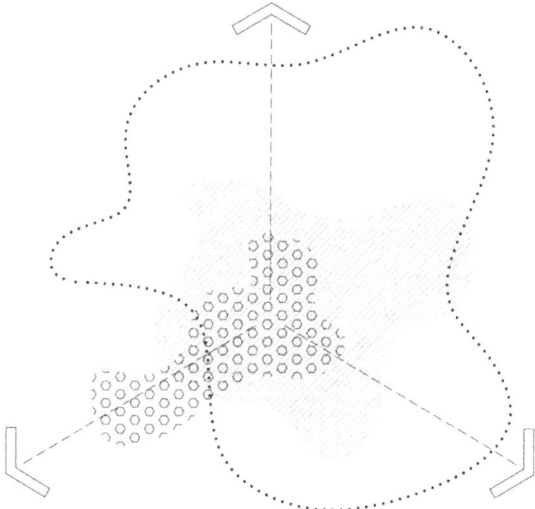

Notes:
- spatial scales are inconsistent, overlapping and affected by multiple factors. Conventional equilibrium-based Venn and pillar constructs of sustainability do not take this into account. Consequently, efficiency driven approaches are limited in their capacity to respond to spatial scale and the socio-cultural behaviours that influence it.

Culturally responsive analysis allows us to evaluate existing and future spatial conditions. In doing so, it also grants us an understanding of the value of 'missing' infrastructures, not simply as absences, but as a lacuna for opportune introduction of capacity to facilitate societal benefit.

This chapter explores, presents and discusses several design-led approaches for culturally responsive analysis which views sustainable architecture as part of a complex network of nested scales; including renewable energy and urban configuration. Tensions and conflicts embedded in the application of efficiency-driven design are exposed and compared with effective sustainable design approaches which tackle interconnected and cross-thematic social, cultural, economic and environmental conditions. This highlights that culturally responsive analysis – as opposed to environmental accounting models – can recognize and materialize the often intangible dimension of *effectiveness* in sustainable design. The projects discussed here argue that creating environmental preconditions to support sustainable behaviour is critical to achieving effective sustainable outcomes and that this can be done through data analysis and spatial mapping that locates human activity in place and culture. Culturally responsive analysis can expend our understanding of the limits of urban space by identifying novel behaviours and patterns of use.

EFFICIENCY: TENSIONS BETWEEN SPATIAL SCALE AND METRICS

There is a large body of theory and practice that attempts to both describe and represent sustainability in architecture and the built environment as an idea, realising it as a type of formal built object and technologically proficient tool. Observing how factors driving sustainable design are integrated into the work processes of architects and designers exposes tensions between the theory and practice of sustainability. Further tensions exist between ideas and characteristics of local/particular and global/universal applications and realities of sustainable design produced by deterministic practices. While objective-based, deterministic practices are able to provide measurable outcomes to specific criteria, they are limited in their ability to respond to the complex social practices that overlay, interface and shape the physical environment. The goal of producing strong overlaps or, indeed, full convergences of these themes is rarely achieved, and a tendency to separate and isolate them results in significant disconnects between the theory and practice of sustainability. At the core of this disconnection is the issue of how sustainability is often defined and addressed as a matter of technological performance and not a cultural challenge. One of the key problems of sustainability is that its definition and meaning can change widely from interpreter to interpreter (Coucill, 2013). This makes it quite difficult to put forward a singular, clearly defined answer to the question of what sustainability actually is.

Tensions emerge when the outcomes of efficiency-driven sustainable design are situated in a wider context. This broader scale not only includes environmental conditions, but a more complex landscape of socio-cultural behaviours that influence and shape spatial conditions and performance. Technology is increasingly adopted as a responsive tool in this context; one which is able to capture and process greater qualities of data with the intention of informing responsive outcomes to conditions as they emerge. However, does the increasing complexity of metrics and data really represent lived experience or respond to culturally embedded behaviours?

Integrating sustainability in design processes

Sustainability is an established core principle of architectural and built environment practice. It is acknowledged in national and international laws and treaties and manifests in professional qualification criteria for architects. In determining what sustainability means in the built environment, preference is given to metric-based approaches to auditing spaces (whether internal or external), that are driven by overarching assessment frameworks, such as LEED or BREEAM. These methods predominantly focus on performance efficiency and have become embedded as key stages of the work processes relating to the design and realisation of built form (Gunder, 2006), displacing them from their intended use as post-realisation evaluation tools.

Full integration of sustainable design assessment methods into design processes has received both praise and criticism. Carmona & Dann (2007) and Carmona (2009) note a rise in support for supplementary codes in planning policy. Often, these are place-specific codes, written with the intention of creating desirable places that can be commodified. Collado-Ruiz & Ostad-Ahmad-Ghorabi (2010) articulate that the need to address sustainability issues has led to the unquestioned application of performance-based objectives, without any indication of their efficacy or how they reconcile with the processes of the designers that formalise them.

Some studies of creative processes suggest that objectives are detrimental to design. (Clevenger & Haymaker, 2011; Collado-Ruiz & Ostad-Ahmad-Ghorabi, 2010; Ross, 2012) There is, however, evidence culled from the perspective of design practice that suggests objective-driven processes can assist distributed decision making by serving as a shared language and set of common goals for groups of professionals and non-professionals working together on complex problems. (Cooper, et al., 2009; Guy & Moore, 2007; Imrie & Street, 2011; Lombardi, et al., 2011) A more accurate description of the implications of sustainability assessment methods for architectural and built environment design is that they are design-leading, rather than design-led. This means that in some circumstances, they can provide a contingency for practitioners to justify their design approaches. (Coucill, 2013)

Efficiency In and Of Itself

It is important to recognise that the approaches outlined above are specific to the immediate spatial scale of the building or landscape to which they apply. Sustainability, however, does not adhere to the definitive site boundaries of building projects in the same way that efficiency-driven approaches do. This gives rise to a disconnect between space and dynamic context. Spatial scale is used to define a given area within which multiple interdependent variables act. Through measurable approaches that focus predominantly on spatial performance efficiency--whether at the scale of the room, building, urban area, city, region or beyond--auditing methods for sustainable design neglect to recognise both the complex, dynamic relationships between spaces and their implications beyond defined boundaries.

Auditing methods for sustainability are most easily applied at the scale of the building, which is characterised by variables more easily isolated from the complex social and cultural environment in which the building exists. The simplest way to conceptualize this is by imagining an isolated room within a building, where the alignment between heating and cooling requirements and predicted occupancy schedules inform strategies for energy efficiency. Within this space, there are a limited number of variables and activity affecting performance, and the number of possible changes can be predicted with some level of certainty, thereby defining the number of possible outcomes and solutions for efficiency in a given area, such as energy consumption. Buildings, however, do not exist in a vacuum. Spaces encompassing complex urban and environmental conditions involve a much greater number of interdependent variables. The combination of dynamic conditions and countless actions makes it increasingly challenging to apply targeted metrics to performance with any certainty. The disconnection of the small scale from any form of larger context neglects other factors informing use, value and obsolescence, potentially displacing efficiency achieved in isolation.

Framing Efficiency

Market forces and trends shape how sustainable space is captured, identified and recognised through formal qualities of the built environment.

Performance efficiency is also a shifting paradigm, which, as expected, responds to emerging knowledge in the field. New methods, apparatus for measurement and developments in understanding best practice, help to advance how the issue of scale and dynamism is conceptualized. Consequently, auditing methods vary depending on trends and how objectives and performance criteria are selected. Recognising the complexity of the built environment as a space for social activity, performance metrics aim to quantify qualitative conditions through compromise and comparison. Parameters for some evaluation models of pre- and post-occupancy performance testing reveal tensions between intended design and actual use. Deviation from expected dynamics ultimately affects the predictions on which efficient performance is based. This raises the question of whether building users should be educated about how a space is correctly used, as unanticipated use might impact the performance metrics of a code-compliant building and lead to premature obsolescence.

Further tensions between the conception, operation and performance of the sustainable space are manifest in how some assessment methods allow for the trade-off of credits between category benchmarks to accommodate flexibility. For example, a design may not be compliant in one category but may attain more credits in an alternative one to compensate. (BREEAM New Construction, 2011, pp.19-27) Such offsetting exposes paradoxes where buildings exhibiting significant spatial overproduction can still score highly on metrics of sustainability. The 1400m^2 RIBA House of the Year 2017 (Wright & Maxwell, 2017) is a good example of this, having met the highest Level 6 of the Code for Sustainable Homes (an assessment method withdrawn by the Government in England since 2015) and achieved an 'A' rated Energy Performance Certificate, (a calculation based on material assumptions to estimate annual CO_2 emission and energy used per m^2). What this suggests is that the articulation of sustainability has now become so abstracted from actual use that almost any code-compliant building can be deemed sustainable to a degree. A widespread auditing-based approach to sustainability is an extension of a metric based system where measurements are derived and ranked against a known set of parameters. This quantum-based approach can be used as a frame to score actual outputs and use against narrow sets of criteria. It also sets up a context where high performance in one area can mask or actively reduce performance in another. This is inherently a product of evaluating efficiency at predefined, isolated spatial scales.

Data in Efficiency Driven Design

If the problem with metrics is that space is dynamic and larger areas of built environment; neighborhoods, towns and cities, are more difficult to predict, then the answer so far has been to capture a greater extent of the variables at play through the integration of technology that enables constant monitoring of performance efficiency. This technology is increasingly prevalent at all scales and in all environments, from buildings to infrastructure and public spaces, operating in the form of sensors, meters and networked communication devices.

Distributed, connected, digitally-enabled technology captures data with the capacity to expose patterns of social, economic, political and environmental interaction with the physical world, offering opportunities to process, evaluate and react to prevailing conditions. Some argue that the real-time analysis of this *big data* enables "new modes of urban governance, and provides the raw material for envisioning and enacting more efficient, sustainable, competitive, productive, open and transparent cities" (Kitchin, 2014, p.1). The now widespread production of data is thought to potentially overcome the challenges of responding to perpetual built environment use changes.

Vast, manifold data sets, however, are not benign or objective and can be limited in their capacity to respond to some of the more subtle, social and cultural complexities of producing sustainable spaces. Data capture can emphasise "micro scale interactions between architecture and human behavior" and can produce "the deterministic interpretation of people-environment relationships" (Knox, 2007, pp. 114-115; Gutman et al., 2010)[1].

Access to data and the ease of generating greater quantities of data from more accurate sources offers opportunities to make better decisions for sustainable development. Data production is also presented as providing more equitable opportunities to engage and participate in the formulation of policies and planning decisions which affect the public realm. This appears to be an improvement on past strategies where information was protected and decisions were controlled by an elite. (Batty et al., 2012) However, although open access to data is increasingly possible and considered advantageous as part of the design process, there is no universal approach to interaction with it, and citizens are open to engage in passive and active capacities. Therefore it does not necessarily achieve decision making that is more democratic or equitable. One can argue that it is now simply an alternative elite who controls the data: with large corporations driving the integration of technology in contemporary society.

It is important to acknowledge that data exists as a consequence "of the ideas, techniques, technologies, people and contexts that conceive, produce, process, manage, analyse and store them" (Kitchin, 2014, p.8, following Bowker and Star 1999; Lauriault, 2012; Ribes & Jackson, 2013). Data is a "product of choices and constraints, shaped by a system of thought, technical know-how, public and political opinion, ethical considerations, the regulatory environment, and funding and resourcing" (Kitchin, 2014, p.9) and does not always take into consideration underpinning values and interests (Kitchin, 2014). The assumption that data is

---

[1] Also see (Saint, 1983)

unbiased ignores the contingency and context of the data itself as well as the idiosyncrasies of the people and places it represents.

Increasing Quantities of Data

The representation of data and the transferability of findings to different contexts can be equally problematic. Patterns can be easily obscured through careful selection and isolation of data, and the universal application of findings derived in this way presents a challenge for local/particular identity. On the one hand, at the local/particular scale, this could indicate movement towards a spatial equality which transcends conventional land value systems. On the other, however, the smoothness of digital space, free from the implications of borders, terrain, topography or distance, could represent a further step toward the homogenisation of physical space.

The premise that data and technology can generate adaptable and responsive qualities through digital layers has attracted the moniker *Smart* and led to the idea that sustainability and smartness are increasingly synonymous. (Garau & Pavan, 2018) However, in such complex circumstances, some level of compromise is inevitable. de Jong, et al. (2015) note that the difference between esoteric initiatives, auditing methods and definitions of sustainable design indicate which trade-offs are more likely. Some authors argue that space "(…) can only be smart if there are intelligence functions that are able to integrate and synthesise this data to some purpose [such as] ways of improving the efficiency, equity, sustainability and quality of life in cities" (Batty et al. 2012). Without considering wider relationships, technology's ability to adapt and respond is limited by data selection, methods of analysis and pre-programmed response, reinforcing dependence on performance metrics. One obvious example of this disconnection is the limited capacity of metrics to effectively describe spatial conditions. This can be seen in how spreadsheets of data do not visually represent the prevailing spatial character they are intended to describe.

Smartness: Widening the Disconnection with Place

It is clear that digital infrastructure is becoming fully interwoven with the physical built environment and that the integration of this technology into urban space is producing novel environments, substantially different from anything we have previously experienced. (Batty, et al., 2012, p.482) The contrast between the ephemeral quality of digital data and the tangibility of real space creates a tension between physical and virtual environments. The designed response to intangible networks and flows requires the cultural location of digital and virtual to enable their effective framing by designed space and architecture.

The tensions identified above expose that the current discourse concerning sustainability is dominated by technocentric and governance strategies, with a lack of reflection on the role of design and the relationship between digital networks and physical space. Spanning multiple levels and scales, at the core of the agenda is achieving efficiency in routine functions, such as energy use, and infrastructural components and systems, such as buildings and transport networks.

Performance metrics however, appear to be myopic in their approach to establishing long-term, culturally responsive places and reducing obsolescence. This is because the manifestation of sustainability as a process of auditing and measuring building performance disconnects architecture from the wider urban and built environment networks that situate it. Deakin (2014, p.219) argues that "our current embedded understanding of intelligence and smart cities puts us on the verge of cultivating a new environmental determinism". Is this the smart sustainable future we once envisioned?

In order to overcome the limitations of existing auditing and sustainability assessment methods, scale must be addressed.

> "Whether we think of the large-scale technological fixes at the core of many contemporary ecological urbanist approaches at one end of the scale, or the back-to-nature philosophies of more traditional green building advocates [...] an over-emphasis on efficiency [in sustainable design] might in fact impede the success of either approach" (Goodbun, 2012, p.54).

This condition demands the re-imagination of smart sustainability in a way which embraces the idea that buildings are components in much wider networks. Similarly, Cooper et al. (2009, p.viii) suggest that "Ultimately, the users of urban environments create or erode sustainability, with the physical, social and economic infrastructures forming the 'places' that locate lifestyles. Therefore, for sustainability interventions to succeed, a human-centered approach must be adopted". New methods of analysis are therefore needed to re-connect sustainability and society through the environments they share.

EFFECTIVENESS: CULTURALLY RESPONSIVE ANALYSIS

Inhabited space, whether urban or otherwise, is made up of layers of complex networks. Various forms of analysis over time have revealed patterns of activity made manifest in the physical environment (Marshall, 2009). These patterns are the product of social and cultural behaviours. Emerging tensions, exacerbated by the disconnection between data and lived experience, which eludes boundaries and specified scales, cannot be addressed by increasing the quantity or complexity of data without first addressing its connection with place.

The design and planning of cities is based on long term analysis of historical precedents and the re-evaluation of situated social, political, economical and environmental needs. This process has been de-railed by ephemeral digital data production and real-time responses of efficiency-driven sustainability which cannot realistically be met by the comparatively static qualities of the built environment. Recognising and responding to scalar complexity for the purposes of sustainable design requires the abstract nature of data to be reconciled with spatial character and quality. It also requires this reconciliation to allow the value of existing spatial conditions to be understood in order to identify opportunities to add value and improve effectiveness.

Effective sustainability, therefore, demands spatial analysis that merges, across a range of scales, the long-term evolution of spatial conditions with the dynamic and reactive context of digitally enabled space. Cultural presence can be viewed as the condition that frames this context, while infrastructure ('Infra' being derived from the Latin 'below'), can be considered an underpinning part of the urban condition which crosses boundaries and services all aspects of society and culture. Viewed through this framework, methods of culturally responsive analysis could support the production of effectively sustainable space.

Meaningful Representation

The importance of cultural presence as a factor in designing infrastructure can be seen in the responses to previous 'invisible' urban phenomena including, sanitation, pollution and energy use. When invisible phenomena become visible as problems, a retrospective response is demanded.

An example of this appears when one re-evaluates the public's relationship with power and energy infrastructure. In post-WWII Britain, the objective for the newly nationalised electricity sector was to construct large generating stations out of the city and away from residential populations, feeding into the National Grid. The introduction of transmission networks dramatically re-shaped public recognition of energy infrastructure and produced a cultural disconnection between building and function. Building typologies shaped by 19th-century power engineering, which located power production within cities and alongside rivers, close to the sources of greatest demand, were rendered technically obsolete. Ironically, this has highlighted the importance of their architecture as an asset for cultural re-appropriation. Their transition from technically obsolete to culturally valuable has driven development of cultural and social spaces at a range of scales, from Bankside Power Station becoming Tate Modern in London to converted electricity sub-station coffee shops in Sydney (Figure 4.2). These realise the latent value of built form through an articulation of the heritage properties of the architecture and reinforce the value of embedding cultural significance or the potential for 'future heritage' in schemes as part of a wider sustainability strategy.

Today, networks distributing large-scale outputs to consumers are becoming increasingly incompatible with decentralised, responsive 21st century renewable technologies. This is evident in the difficulties the National Grid is facing trying to capture fluctuating energy production from renewables with inconsistent outputs, which is triggering consideration of re-localising energy production. The disconnection of form from function that was initially enabled by removing the means of production from view has now allowed for meaning and use to be ascribed to architecture in a fluid, dynamic way. It has also demonstrated the subsidiary importance of technical performance as a way of representing meaning in the built environment, where architectural form, space and material quality are prioritized over function.

Figure 4.2 Electricity sub-station building converted into Coffee Shop, Alexandria, Sydney NSW

Notes:
- Photos © Coucill, L (2018)

The inability of technically measured efforts to reduce energy demand indicates that the scale of the energy problem can no longer be addressed by the energy sector's current strategies. A change in the popular view of energy production and consumption is needed. This calls for a meaningful representation of sustainability, not simply as an absence, but as a culturally valuable and visible component of built form and human behaviours.

Culturally Responsive Analysis

Methods of spatially representing data, coupled with the use of design as a tool for exploration and simulation, have the capacity to identify the conditions and opportunities arising from efficiency-driven metrics and make insightful proposals for effective sustainability. Visual representation of data can be made meaningful in terms of the area it affects, the current and potential conditions it produces, and identifying the current performance it provides in addition to potential capacity. The further step of spatially mapping data allows the cross-examination of spatially embedded themes that represent social and cultural behaviours and their effect at a range of scales, from the local to the global.

This culturally responsive approach to analysis offers three principle opportunities for understanding how the spatial characterisation of data can offer insights into emerging spatial characters that otherwise might not be understood until manifest in the landscape. This exposes a distinction between space and behaviour in the built environment, which is inherently a long-term project, with real-time, on-demand operation and performance. Ultimately, a more culturally-focused approach to spatial analysis reconciles lived experience with efficiency-driven metrics to provide insights into possibilities for effective sustainable spatial design.

The Spatial Characterisation of Data

Visual representation creates a meaningful relationship between data and space. This is particularly useful where local and particular interventions need to be compared with regional, and perhaps global demands. An example of this can be seen in Figure 4.3: a drawing produced to compare the spatial requirements of wind and solar energy. The drawing represents the absolute minimum spatial requirements for each renewable energy source. In this case, the visual representation of the spatial requirement to meet the energy demands of 100 dwellings exposes the cultural and environmental challenges of reconciling power supply and demand with geographic area, visual amenity and underlying infrastructural requirements.

Figure 4.3 Infrastructure Space: An examination of the spatial requirements for wind and solar energy in the Scottish Highland region

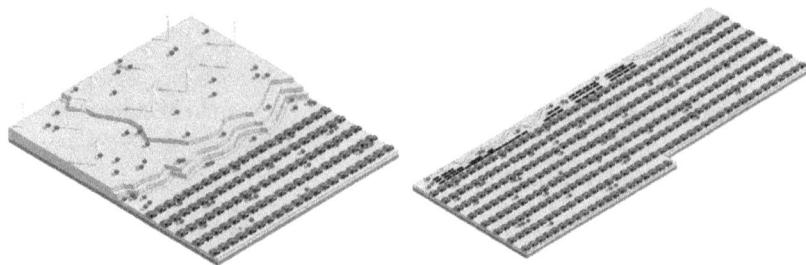

Notes:
- spatial requirements for 100 houses powered by (left) onshore wind and (right) photovoltaic panels
- by Peter Chinnock, Richard Durber, Phil Gannon, Diane Kwan, Mihayla Mihaylova, Sam Power (2016) Manchester School of Architecture supervised by Jefferies, Brook, Coucill, Csepely-Knorr & Morton.

Figure 4.4 Infrastructure Space: An examination of the spatial relationship between renewable energy production and demand in Cornwall

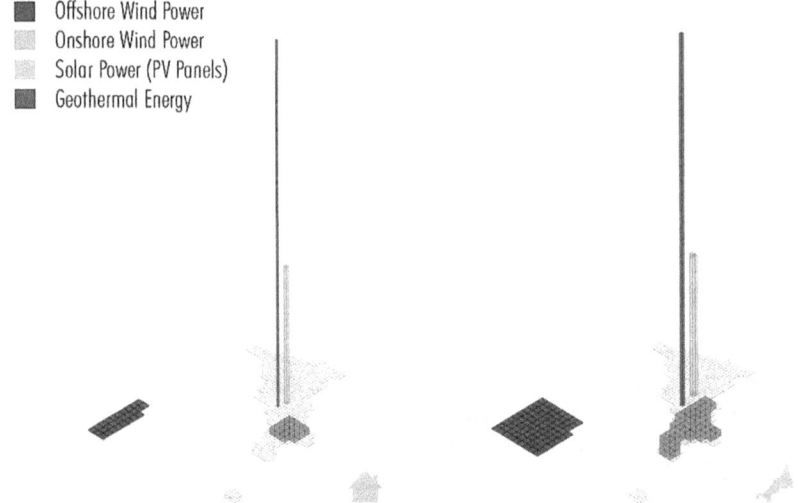

Notes:
- (left) footprint required to produce Cornwall's total domestic yearly energy consumption, (right) footprint required to produce Cornwall's total yearly energy consumption
- by Eva Nella, Connor Armitage, Tom Fantom, Antoine Louchet (2017) Manchester School of Architecture supervised by Jefferies, Coucill, Morton & Csepely-Knorr.

A similar example is the thematic analysis of the county of Cornwall, UK, which unites energy demand data for the region with the spatial footprint of renewables (Figure 4.4). Using average spatial requirements for siting renewable sources and appraising the capacity of land's potential for multi-functionality, data regarding the domestic and industrial requirements for the region can be mapped in ways that readily communicate the spatial efficiency and impact of renewable energy types.

Conventional modes of graphical data representation are typically produced for singular, specific audiences. The complexities of urban and built environment space, however, affect, a wide range of audiences and thus should be easily legible. Architects and urban designers are well equipped to use their acute understanding of space not only to examine spatial data but represent it in a format that can contribute to the on-going discourse. The visual and spatial representation of data acts as a tool with which to question, test and generate hypotheses about future spatial conditions.

Re-evaluating Spatial Character

What should smart cities look like, and how should they characterise space? The omnipresence of connected digital devices and infrastructure is changing socio-economic behaviours. The idea of a reciprocal relationship between human behavior and activity and the production of tools is long-standing. It is clear that socio-economic behaviour is changing as a product of digital tools and the way in which transactions are undertaken remotely with the increasing popularity of online retail. These emerging conditions have huge, currently undefined implications for the operation and performance of urban space that are yet to be fully manifest in the formal and physical qualities of the built environment. Increasing vacancy of UK retail space provides evidence of this, directly impacting urban quality.

Data representation techniques and spatial analysis were used to explore these conditions in the region of the Scottish Highland. They identified that, although the region is typically considered to be rural, it displayed characteristics of urban behaviour through the mechanisms of digital infrastructure. Methods of representation and analysis allowed for the re-evaluation of spatial character, posing the question; 'What are the limits of the contemporary city?'.

Figure 4.5 provides an example of the spatial analysis and data representation that led to this. The work was conducted to examine local and regional implications of visible and invisible infrastructure and revealed that some of the most remote and sparsely populated areas of the UK are able to operate in the same capacity as high-density cities.

Figure 4.5 Infrastructure Space: Dispersed Urban network analysis of the Scottish Highland region in 2015/16

Notes:
- by Tanya Ittan, Georgina Mitchell, Nicholas Nilsen, George Thomson, Jessica Weeks (2016) Manchester School of Architecture supervised by Jefferies, Brook, Coucill, Csepely-Knorr & Morton.

In this work, the combined effect of recognising buildings as components of an expanded network and the speed, acceleration and intersection of digital and physical mobility reframes the idea of a city. Urban tendencies become apparent where urban operations adopt the appearance of rural space, giving rise to the phenomenon of the *Hyper-Dispersed City*. Spatial analysis allowed conventional definitions of urban space, which assume high levels of density as a characteristic feature, to be challenged. The work recognised that conventional definitions ignored the behaviour of inhabitants within the identified region and exposed that it is possible for inhabitants of sparsely occupied space to behave in highly urban ways that bear little traditional connection to the place-specific forms of behaviour that would be implied by conventional readings of rural space.

Such findings are wholly reliant on the spatial representation of data and only become evident when traditional metrics of urban space, such as population density, are replaced by metrics that observe the behaviours and use of digital space. For example, the Scottish Highland region has a population density of 9ppl/km^2. This is the lowest in the UK, whose metropolitan areas have significantly higher population densities, such as Edinburgh's 1800ppl/km^2 and London Islington's 14500ppl/km^2. However, by viewing populations through the lens of digital behaviours and their use of digital services, such as online shopping and access to next day delivery networks, distance and thereby population density becomes less significant. We are currently witnessing a paradigm shift where technology and networking have begun allowing new forms of usage to interact with traditional style places. Highland region presents us with a spatial condition that has been shaped by rural processes to *appear* rural but that is now occupied in a way that has enabled dispersed uses and characteristically urban behaviours. Such critical reframing enables the sustainable potential of a dispersed territory within a comparator set of more conventional dense settlement types. This is useful from both a policy-making and performance perspective when developing critically grounded proposals and operational models.

Accommodating Longevity in a Real-time Context

The identification and definition of critical problems located in geographic, cultural and historic contexts is the starting point for enabling the design process to address spatial shifts. Data production used to inform short-term, automated responses in smart spaces is key to understanding the development of use and occupation patterns as part of long-term appraisal plans. This approach cross-references data regarding the complex, interconnected use, performance and operation of services, networks and space made manifest through place-specific historic and cultural practices. Both multi-level and multi-agent-based systems are as yet unable to grasp the esoteric qualities and conditions of space, nor the complex cultural activities that affect it.

Existing precedents have provided insights into established socio-economic traits. As demonstrated by the case of the Scottish Highland, it is possible to illustrate formerly invisible characteristics and implications of social behaviours for the physical environment. This is an example of the distinction between the performance (a real-time factor) and appearance (a long-term effect) of physical space. Digital networks, in conjunction with physical infrastructures, have enabled places to retrospectively behave in the manner of a conceptual city. Appropriating the language of the ideal allows the reality of a place to be repositioned. An example of this can be seen in Cornwall's potential reading as a contextualized model of the Garden City. Initially proposed by Ebenezer Howard (1898), this idealized urban model is focused on achieving ideal proximities and spatial relationships between amenities to achieve operational space and deliver an ideal lifestyle. Though Cornwall was not built as a Garden City, it has evolved towards performing like a Garden City. The diagram of Cornwall Garden City (Figure 4.6) positions the urban space of the county within a conceptual urban model, challenging its popular framing as an essentially rural space. This exemplifies the way the space performs, made evident in the cross-thematic mapping of socio-economic data, physical and digital infrastructures.

Figure 4.6 Infrastructure Space: Cornwall Garden City. Connectivity and Networks analysis of Cornwall and the Isles of Scilly

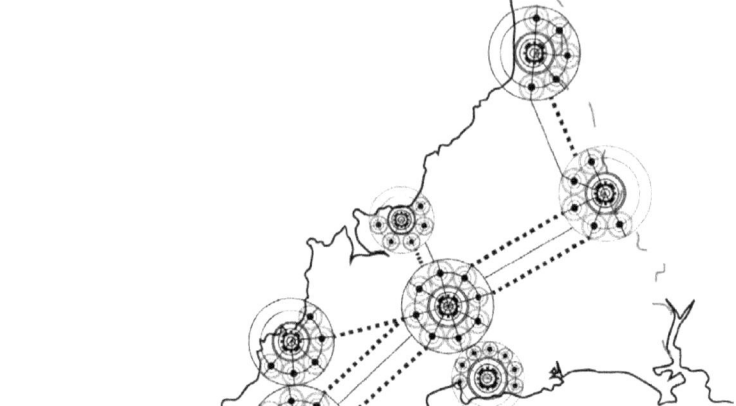

Notes:
- by Peter Bell, Kotryna Dapsyte, Stephen Morris, Morgan Wild (2017) Manchester School of Architecture supervised by Jefferies, Coucill, Morton & Csepely-Knorr.

LIVED EXPERIENCE: RECONNECTING DATA AND SPACE

Mapping data across a range of core themes is essential to developing a deeper understanding of lived experience. Incorporating design into the representation and exploration of data not only exposes a deeper understanding of the operational context of space, but also provides informed insights into development requirements. This comprises an alternative and unique approach to the current speculative market, which often produces generic high-specification space that, while generic, is not flexible, nor capable of meeting the needs of specific occupants (Moe, 2013). The use of design to model and demonstrate spatial qualities is a tool that, if it is not simply overlooked, is appreciated only as a means of representing the formal qualities of pre-determined, market informed developments in the built environment. Representing architectural proposals through various forms of media now interfaces with digital technology to provide opportunities for critically assessing proposals prior to construction.

Design as a mechanism for effectiveness

Culturally responsive analysis generates knowledge that enables us to identify appropriate spatial relationships, materials and structures for intervention. It also provides us an understanding of the socio-economic and cultural implications thereof. The design of space should not be de-laminated from the multifaceted context in which it exists. An early example of developing this approach can be seen in Maccreanor Lavington Architects et al.'s winning entry to the 2006 Whitefield Housing international competition. (Figure 4.7). In their scheme, a combination of significant tactical and technical performance upgrades, including thermal performance improvements and hidden refuse disposal, were introduced into an area of dense heritage-listed 19th-century housing. These changes were supported at a neighbourhood level by the repurposing of backyards into shared gardens and the strategic insertion of a biofuel power plant that provided a district heating system in the form of a new urban park (Logan et al., 2008).

Figure 4.7 Winning scheme, Whitefield Housing international Housing Competition (2006). Whitefield, Nelson, UK

Notes:
- by Maccreanor Lavington Architects with Jefferies & Keeffe et al.

Maccreanor Lavington's project demonstrated that through a considered engagement with technical performance demands within the scope of a human-centered approach to realising functional urban space, opportunities to create infrastructures of sustainability with binary benefits emerge (Keeffe & Jefferies, 2011). This is a strategy that deliberately spatializes sustainability (in the form of a public park) whilst also creating 'Future Heritage' conditions for cultural appropriation of sustainable power infrastructure and built form, rather than viewing heritage as a retrospective aspect of the built environment. Ideas proposed in this propositional scheme have subsequently been realised by the architects in award-winning projects including Ryle Yard, Cambridge and Dujardin Mews, London.

Design for identifying opportunity

Culturally responsive analysis relies on design activity to prioritize investigatory work and identify design opportunities which reconcile the unique cultural conditions of place with global, national and local objectives for sustainability.

Figure 4.8 Infrastructure Space: Patterns of Power - Visualising pattern types which generate cultural landscapes; buildings augment and reveal latent contextual correlations.

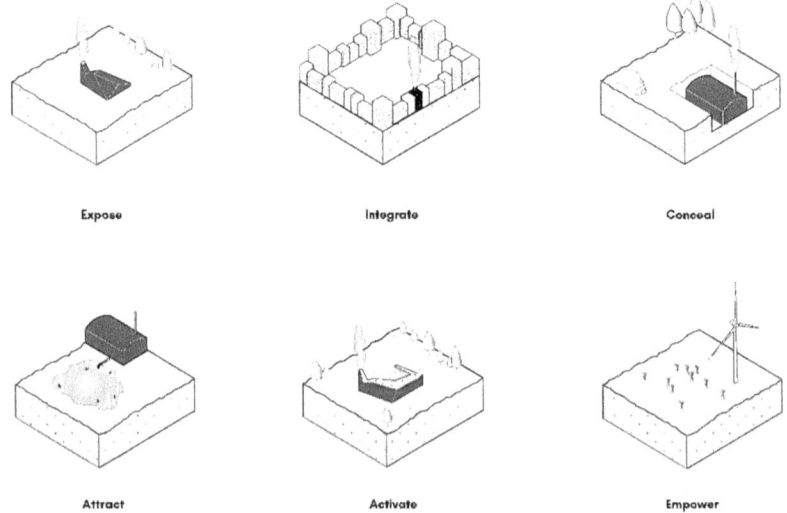

Notes:
- by Evagelia Nella (2018) Manchester School of Architecture supervised by Jefferies, Coucill, Morton & Csepely-Knorr.

Recognising effectiveness 89

'Patterning Power' (Figure 4.8) explores the architectural representation of energy infrastructure made possible by design research and cross-thematic analysis of extant data sets. Spatial Analysis revealed correlations between energy demand and socio-economic deprivation in specific areas within Cornwall, UK, a region which has yet to capitalise on its geothermal capacity. Footprints of energy generation were compared (Figure 4.5) to reveal that a geothermal plant is efficient in terms of both power density and appropriate to vernacular scale. This, coupled with the introduction of advanced renewable energy production and smart grid distribution networks that can mediate the adverse impacts of energy production, opens up design opportunities that require a reassessment of society's relationship with infrastructural typologies. When a contemporary power station sits in the city, not beyond its periphery, what does it need to look like? The redefinition of energy production as a clean renewable process at the level of a local or microgrid enables, once again, a rethinking of the power station as an urban element within the context of contemporary infrastructural knowledge and theory. This demands that power production buildings are no longer simply engineered facilities, but rather components of an urban architecture.

- Responding to the combination of place-specific, cultural, typological and technical requirements, the project used estimations based on population densities and power demand to apply Christopher Alexander's *Pattern Language* (1977) concepts to the Cornish case for renewable energy production. This embodied the scales and patterns at regional district, urban and local levels, as a radical approach to integrating renewable energy and urban regeneration. The result is a 'cultural landscape' that avoids considering power production buildings as isolated objects and instead views them as patterns that augment contextual correlations. These correlations are used to redefine an existing defunct urban space as a significant point of arrival and production, experienced as part of the city from both land and sea. The proposed building is a hybrid typology, using contemporary theory to fuse 21st Century infrastructure and cultural space in response to long-term data analysis and produce a socio-technically generated architecture (Figure 4.9).

Figure 4.9 Infrastructure Space: Patterns of Power - Geo-thermal power plant, Penzance UK

Notes:
- by Evagelia Nella (2018) Manchester School of Architecture supervised by Jefferies, Coucill, Morton & Csepely-Knorr.

CONCLUSIONS: THE RECOGNITION AND REPRESENTATION OF 'SUSTAINABILITY'

The projects presented highlight that efficiency-led, target-driven approaches to sustainable architecture are not necessarily commensurate with lived-experiences, exposed through cross-thematic data-mapping. Rather, sustainable design creates the preconditions to support sustainable behaviour. This means considering sustainable architecture as part of a complex network spanning nested local/particular and global/universal scales, informed by dynamic socioeconomic and cultural behaviour. The projects discussed argue that this is one of the main means for achieving effective sustainable outcomes and that this can be done through data analysis and spatial mapping that locates human activity in place and culture. Capturing and representing data must be considered essential to developing measurably positive designed outcomes. Culturally responsive analysis has expended our understanding of the limits of urban space by identifying novel behaviours and patterns of use. This has disassociated the description of a space (e.g., as 'rural' or 'urban') from its appearance or density of occupation. It has also facilitated designed responses to spatial and societal conditions that can be captured to provide a basis on which to make designs that respond to a real, measurable reality rather than just an image.

Culturally responsive analysis and design is a tool that enables one to explore the tensions existing between ideas and characteritics of the local/particular and global/universal, such as the difference in approach between technical and sociotechnical practices. Whilst advanced technical performance is desirable, it is not the most important prerequisite for sustainability in the built environment. Through considered engagement of technical aspects of sustainability with a wider sociotechnical understanding of space, it is possible to design new forms of urban space and new structures of urbanism that address demands by means that are resilient and adaptable. Culturally responsive analysis and design attempts to unpack the complexity of contemporary sustainability with thematic, cross referenceable lines of enquiry. This creates an opportunity to recognise competing agendas and requires the user to make value judgements around the application of the findings. This is an approach that reflects the lived experience and real complexity of applied sustainable decision making and exposes unexpected ways that differing factors of spatial occupation can affect sustainable outcomes.

Embedding Policy

The cultural perception of sustainable space is one of the most challenging aspects for contemporary policy, technical and design practitioners to reconcile. The dangers of overreliance on the representation of measurable, technological and quantifiable progress can be seen in earlier collapses of confidence in progress, such as the crisis of Modernism in the 1970s.

The discrediting of universal aspects of progress is still playing out in our contemporary cultural context, which now questions the very idea of 'truth'. In recognising that there are many readings of a singular situation, it is possible to develop proposals and architectural solutions that embody both advanced technology and culturally resonant forms. This is a deliberate strategy to produce resilience and support change over time.

Effective policymaking depends on proper research and evidence-based decision making in order to achieve its goals. Producing data that is accurate, legible and applicable often proves problematic for this, however. Policy is often abstract, intended to create positive outcomes through actions situated in dynamic, shifting contexts. The architect, urban planner, engineer or designer is faced with a challenge to synthesise policy objectives, often through a codified form of delivery, to develop and deliver a high-quality built environment that responds to policy.

The extent to which definitions of high quality built environment schemes vary becomes apparent when one reviews the results of professionally aligned prizes for excellence. Architectural, engineering and planning professions will tend to choose very different examples of excellence when identifying best practice. This difference of opinion is reflected in the lack of consistency evident in the current debate around sustainability and is a challenge to producing a unified approach to delivering schemes that are both sustainable and resilient. It is clear that this is a global objective, however, as ongoing research is taking place in Canada. (Chupin et al., 2018)

Supporting 'Smart'

The emergence and adoption of smart technologies in the operation and design of contemporary urban space presents a challenge to all aspects of governance, urban design, and everyday human behaviour. These technologies are often presented as a means of resolving the dynamic challenges of the city. However, is the city a problem that can be solved? By using available special and infrastructural environments to respond intelligently to societal need , it is possible to enhance the current operation and engagement of all types of space and to enable citizens to access assets by choice rather than necessity.

A complex understanding of a place through data mapping enables the identification of latency within a situation, i.e., the potential for it to be developed towards a variety of different outcomes. This may be the result of types of either realised or potential surplus (e.g., renewable energy capacity), or the result of two or more factors creating synergies. The examples of urban proposals discussed above demonstrate that, through a continuous focus on maximising the potential of place, infrastructural solutions can act as drivers for the creation of inhabitable, measurably good places that embody resilience and indeterminacy as core aspects of their design. We recognise that technological obsolescence is faster than cultural change and that society's view of what is good or bad built form also shifts over time. Consequently, we believe new infrastructures that support the development of urban culture must be able to both accept redundancy as an inevitable part of their lifecycle and embody a potential to support culture as future heritage components and spaces.

Work discussed above in Highland, Cornwall and Nelson demonstrates different facets of this approach. The mass adoption of smart systems will enable networks to become far more responsive and effective, reducing energy use and responding to climate change in ways that are nuanced and multifaceted. This will make a significant shift away from a metric-based assessment context where obviously inefficient and profligate schemes can be ranked a 'outstanding' for energy use. The work discussed here proposes an analysis and design method that embodies interaction and complexity—one which would allow schemes to be understood within a wider context as components of networks, and enables policy and design decisions to be made from an evidential base that is multifaceted and user friendly.

Through the thorough interrogation and questioning of preconceived ideas of spatial efficiency, performance and character we propose that a focus on effectiveness, latency and function will enable designers, policymakers and citizens to co-develop truly sustainable responses to the emerging challenges of resource scarcity and climate change.

REFERENCES

Alexander, C. (1977). *A Pattern Language: Towns, Buildings, Construction.* Oxford University Press.

Batty, M., Axhausen, K. W., Giannotti, F., Pozdnoukhov, A., Bazzani, A., Wachowicz, M., Ouzounis, G., & Portugali, Y. (2012). Smart cities of the future. *The European Physical Journal Special Topics*, *214*(1), 481–518. https://doi.org/10.1140/epjst/e2012-01703-3

Bowker, G. C., & Star, S. L. (1999). *Sorting things out: classification and its consequences.* MIT Press.

Carmona, M. (2009). Design Coding and the Creative, Market and Regulatory Tyrannies of Practice. *Urban Studies*, *46*(12), 2643–2667.

Carmona, M., & Dann, J. (2007). Design Codes. *Urban Design* (101), 16-37.

Clevenger, C. M., & Haymaker, J. (2011). Metrics to assess design guidance. *Design Studies*, *32*(5), 431–456. https://doi.org/10.1016/j.destud.2011.02.001

Chupin, J-P., Adamczyk, G., Cucuzzella, C., Theodore, D., (2018) Architectural Quality for Cultural Institutions in Canada: Shifting Definitions Within Awards of Excellence. Website: https://leap-architecture.org/ Accessed: 12 February 2019

Collado-Ruiz, D., & Ostad-Ahmad-Ghorabi, H. (2010). Influence of environmental information on creativity. *Design Studies*, *31*(5), 479–498. https://doi.org/10.1016/j.destud.2010.06.005

Cooper, R., Evans, G., & Boyko, C. (Eds.). (2009) *Designing Sustainable Cities*. Blackwell Publishing Ltd.

Coucill, L. (2013). Tensions Between Theory and Practice in Architectural Design. PhD. Birmingham Institute of Art and Design.

de Jong, M., Joss, S., Schraven, D., Zhan, C., & Weijnen, M. (2015). Sustainable–smart–resilient–low carbon–eco–knowledge cities; making sense of a multitude of concepts promoting sustainable urbanization. *Journal of Cleaner Production*, *109*, 25–38. https://doi.org/10.1016/j.jclepro.2015.02.004

Deakin, M. (2014). Smart cities: the state-of-the-art and governance challenge. *Triple Helix*, *1*(1), 7. https://doi.org/10.1186/s40604-014-0007-9

Garau, C., & Pavan, V. M. (2018). Evaluating Urban Quality: Indicators and Assessment Tools for Smart Sustainable Cities. *Sustainability*, *10*(3), 575. https://doi.org/10.3390/su10030575

Goodbun, J. (2012, April). An Ecology of Mind. *Architectural Review*, 22–23. https://www.architectural-review.com/essays/an-ecology-of-mind/8628251.article

Gunder, M. (2006). Sustainability: Planning's Saving Grace or Road to Perdition? *Journal of Planning Education and Research*, *26*(2), 208–221. https://doi.org/10.1177/0739456X06289359

Gutman, R., Cuff, D., Wriedt, J., & Bell, B. (Eds.). (2010). *Architecture from the outside in : selected essays*. Princeton Architectural Press. http://site.ebrary.com/id/10452151

Guy, S., & Moore, S. A. (2007). Sustainable Architecture and the Pluralist Imagination. *Journal of Architectural Education*, *60*(4), 15–23. https://doi.org/10.1111/j.1531-314X.2007.00104.x

Howard, E. (1898). *Garden Cities of To-morrow*. Swan Sonnschein & Co.

Imrie, R., & Street, E. (2011). *Architectural Regulation and Design*. Blackwell-Wiley.

Keeffe, G., & Jefferies, T. 2011, 'Future Heritage: is Carbon neutrality possible in historic neighbourhoods?' Paper presented at Energy management in Cultural Heritage, Dubrovnik, Croatia, 01/04/2011 - 01/04/2011, pp. 150-160.

Kitchin, R. (2014). The real-time city? Big data and smart urbanism. *GeoJournal*, *79*(1), 1–14. https://doi.org/10.1007/s10708-013-9516-8

Knox, P. (2007 [1987]) The Social Production of the Built Environment. In M. Carmona, & S. Tiesdell (Eds.), *Urban Design Reader* (pp. 114-125). Architectural Press.

Lauriault, T. P. (2012). *Data, Infrastructures and Geographical Imaginations: Mapping Data Access Discourses in Canada*. PhD Thesis, Carleton University, Ottawa.

Logan, K. et al (2008) CABE HMR Design Task Group 18 (Nelson): Design Task Group Report Sustainable Refurbishment Nelson, Lancashire http://webarchive.nationalarchives.gov.uk/20110118195828/http://www.cabe.org.uk/files/hmr15.pdf

Lombardi, D. R., Caserio, M., Donovan, R., Hale, J., Hunt, D. V. L., Weingaertner, C., Barber, A., Bryson, J. R., Coles, R., Gaterell, M., Jankovic, L., Jefferson, I., Sadler, J., & Rogers, C. D. F. (2011). Elucidating Sustainability Sequencing, Tensions, and Trade-Offs in Development Decision Making. *Environment and Planning B: Planning and Design, 38*(6), 1105–1121. https://doi.org/10.1068/b36161

Marshall, S. (2009). *Cities, Design & Evolution*. Routledge.

Moe, K. (2013). *Convergence: An architectural agenda for energy*. Routledge.

Ribes, D., & Jackson, S. J. (2013). Data bite man: The work of sustaining long-term study. In L. Gitelman (Ed.), *"Raw data" is an oxymoron* (pp. 147–166). MIT Press.

Ross, L. (2012). On contradictory regulations. *Architectural Research Quarterly, 16*(3), 205–209. https://doi.org/10.1017/S1359135513000043

Wright, J. M., & Maxwell, N. (2017). *Caring Wood*. RIBA. https://www.architecture.com/awards-and-competitions-landing-page/awards/riba-regional-awards/riba-south-east-award-winners/2017/caring-wood

CHAPTER 5

EDITORS' PREFACE

In the following essay, Izabel Amaral focusses on the unquantifiable and immaterial dimensions of sustainable architecture. She highlights that the discipline of architecture at its core embodies a tension between the artistic and engineering visions: between the idea and its material manifestation. Founding her arguments on the theory of tectonics, Amaral highlights that any outcome that we see in the real world is a result of a process based on an idea – an idea that preceded the work. The process of making then becomes focused on moving from an idea to an outcome. This requires immaterial senses – encompassing the human hand, craft, the material realities, as well as aesthetic judgments – which she argues are always visible and present in the final outcome. She argues that by repositioning craft, aesthetics and traditional materials at the center of the debate on sustainable architecture, a new paradigm can emerge that allows sustainable buildings to embody immaterial senses, communicate new meanings and reveal the new potentials. Through an example of studio work, the essay exemplifies how the dialectic between artistic visions and the engineering and technical realities can be most successfully negotiated in the making process. The example shows that ideas, craft, and materials become intertwined to create culturally relevant expressions as a dimension of sustainable architecture.

Connections of immaterial to sustainable tectonics

Izabel Amaral

Laurentian University

INTRODUCTION

With the advent of the Anthropocene, architects have begun looking harder than ever before for ways to reduce the environmental impact of buildings. They have begun to address the issue of climate change by rethinking how we use, build and transform our buildings. Since constructing sustainable buildings requires careful use of resources and serious attention to the wellbeing of future inhabitants, it calls for new ways of fabricating, as well as the re-appropriation of traditional building cultures that respect the environment. Because of this, too, there is a great need for discourse concerning craft and craft theories as a relevant measure to be considered in sustainable building practices. Craft is more than simply skillful production. It both participates in the culture and perception of our built environment and harbours a moral concern about the careful use of materials and techniques.

Since Kenneth Frampton's (1995) reawakening of the 19th-century term *Tektonik* in his essential work *Studies in Tectonic Culture*, the ongoing theory of tectonics as a *poetics of construction* has been recognized as a means of thinking about ways to bridge the pragmatic aspects of building on issues related to the culture, aesthetics and phenomenology of architecture. Frampton's work has given rise to subsequent critiques[1] and works that have investigated the phenomenon of tectonics from theoretical standpoint (Chupin & Simonnet, 2005a), and more recently an ecological perspective (Beim & Stylsvig Madsen, 2014).

But how does the theory of tectonics relate to sustainability? Is it possible that tectonics could help designers deal with issues of building culture, aesthetics and sustainability? To answer these questions, we need to understand the factors driving the craft's significance in relation to sustainability.

---

[1] The major critiques being the many essays in the Vol 14 of the magazine *ANY* (published in May 1996) addressing from one side a polyphony of meanings in Frampton's work, or a critique opposing tectonic to digital fabrication.

Sustainable building techniques have traditionally been expressed through the assessment of resources, carbon emissions, or life-cycle analysis, with most results of this taking the form of a direct communication strategy (Beim & Stylsvig Madsen, 2014). The self-explanatory inclusion of visual strategies such as green roofs or solar panels does not necessarily equate to sustainable buildings having values of immaterial quality. In spite of this, however, there are many ways of understanding immateriality, a number of which represent the Platonic notion that ideas precede and are superior to works of art of architecture (Emmons, 2015; Hale, 2000).

Much can be learned from a focused study of the tectonic in relation to the built form — particularly through an investigation of how theoreticians like Gottfried Semper and Kenneth Frampton have addressed issues of sustainability, knowing that material and aesthetic considerations have prevailed over the course the term's long history. The debate surrounding tectonics evokes questions of great pedagogical importance. As Chupin and Simonnet explain, there is a large "disjunction between formal thought and technical thought," and "architecture students are often divided between the legitimacy of the engineer's technical discourse and the fruitfulness of the artist's visual discourse" (Chupin & Simonnet, 2005b). Considering scale in relation to human perception and experience, then, we will now go on to explore tectonics as a fundamental piece of design theory that addresses connections between material and immaterial scales relevant in pedagogical, theoretical and practical contexts.

TECTONICS AND NATURE IN GOTTFRIED SEMPER'S THEORY

Gottfried Semper's theory cannot be separated from the 19th-century German architectural circle, which was dominated by a large interest in construction, considered, then, to be the essence of architecture. Discussions of historical revival and Gothic architecture at the time gave rise to a debate about the notion of style, which also took place in English and French circles. Two prominent topics of debate were Greek architecture, whose principles were supposedly derived from the forms of nature, and Gothic architecture, whose principles were then understood as the exploration of the physical properties of construction. Concerns about a new German architectural style were typically focused on building techniques, new materials like iron and glass, and, above all, references to national identity (Herrmann, 1992). This discussion considered the adaptations of the Greek and Gothic models, consequently raising ethical questions, because mixing the Greek post-and-beam system with a vaulted system appeared to be discrepant from an artistic point of view. For a long time, Heinrich Hübsch's question about the creation of a new German-style remained unanswered. As pointed out by Mallgrave, the discussions of the 19th century lead to a distinction between two fundamental notions, that of *styles* in the plural, to speak of different schools and artistic periods, and that of *style* in the singular, referring to the artistic act taking place in the human intellectual universe (Mallgrave, 1983).

In Karl Wilhelm Bötticher's treatise on architectural ornaments, *Die Tektonik der Hellenen* (1852), tectonic refers to the activity of construction, and more particularly to the activity that elevates construction to the realm of the artistic (Mallgrave, 1983). Bötticher's theory describes architecture as a dynamic and infinite universe of forms, where tectonics articulates function, structure and architecture's symbolic dimension. Bötticher (1992) argues that architectural styles are first defined by the roof system that gives form to the space below. Thus, the creation of a new style depends solely on a new constructive solution. According to Mitchell Schwarzer, however, what Bötticher actually proposes is an actual architectural doctrine comprising four themes: the plan, the roof, the supports, and the spatial relations (Schwarzer, 1993). Bötticher's tectonics refers to a theory of architectural aesthetics, one which assumes that "the beauty of architecture comes exactly from the explanation of the mechanical aspects of the building" (Bötticher, 1852). This theory of aesthetics opposes the Hegelian philosophy of aesthetics, which conceived that art should be free from its material (Schwarzer, 1998). Rejecting the idea that architecture is a minor art form because of its mechanical necessities, the German architect also deplores that the philosophy of aesthetics ignores its material aspects.

Gottfried Semper, with his imposing work, *Der Stil*, published in 1860-63, seeks to give a definitive answer to the debate on the question of style. Semper, however, does not seek to answer Hübsch's question, *In what style should we build?*, nor does he propose a sharp answer to the question *What is style?*. On the contrary, he develops a remarkable theory of style, which implies a new explanation for the origins of architecture. Although *Der Stil* presents itself as a practical aesthetic textbook containing an empirical theory of art, Mallgrave posits that it is rather a theoretical treatise on style that aims to recognize its underlying material and technical conditions (Semper, 2004, p.18). And this titular notion represented Semper's greatest life's goal. As Mallgrave (1983) explains, in the quest for a notion of style, Semper employed a relatively continuous process between 1834 and 1870, transitioning from a technical, materialistic background to an understanding of the themes or basic ideas of works of art. His ultimate definition of style concerns the artistic work and its process. The fact remains that Semper's theory, even if its explanation of the historical origins of art has been questioned, still has a reflective potential that architectural theory is yet to fully embrace. This potential requires a contemporary reinterpretation of his theory, one incorporating his definition of the term tectonics.

Semper's idea that techniques have symbolic connotations can be seen in one particular illustration of an Egyptian engraving. In the engraving, two characters tie a knot around the pharaoh's heart, uniting bundles of papyrus and lotus flowers, which symbolize the unification of Lower and Upper Egypt into one single empire. This image forms part of an argument concerning the knot as an artistic symbol the premise that textiles are the art at the origin of architecture.

The art of tectonics (carpentry) occupies one hundred and forty-one pages of *Der Stil* and is described as the art of building with wood, ranging from small pieces of furniture pieces to full buildings. The notion forms part of the premise that four technical motifs led to the development of architecture and could be used to explain its artistic nature. These four technical motifs – textiles, ceramics, tectonics (carpentry), and stereotomy (stone cutting) – are analyzed in *Der Stil* in terms of their respective relationships to architecture. The book's theory explains the historical evolution of ornaments from their material and technical roots to, eventually, the origins of architecture. For Semper, architecture is not just the explanation of the static properties of construction, but something whose symbolic meaning relates to its technical origins.

Semper identifies four categories of raw materials (or basic materials). They are pliable, like fabric; flexible and malleable, like clay; long and elastic, like wood; and strong and dense, like stone. Each primitive material is considered the ideal medium for a different technique. Fabrics are used for weaving; clay is used for ceramics; wood is used for frameworks; and stone is used for stereotomy. Metallurgy, however, is, classified differently. The premise of the four technical motifs has to do with another important aspect of Semper's theory: the argument of the *four elements of architecture*, present both in *Der Stil* and its eponymous essay (Semper, 1989). These three quartets (materials, motifs and elements) are all a part of Semper's mission to explain the origin of architecture, something which itself coincides with the 19th century's development of archeology. The four elements are defined as the hearth or space (*der Herd*), the podium or the mound (*der Erdaufwurf*), the enclosure (*die Umfriedigung*) and the roof (*das Dach*). In Semper's view, the hearth is *the moral element* of the building. It originates from the *sacred fire* around which men were originally grouped and organized. Semper's four elements would comprise the original archetype of classical architectural forms, an idea illustrated by the famous Caribbean hut. In short, his elements relate to aspects that are simultaneously considered both functional and symbolic. What makes Semper's theory original is that his four elements do not have forms *a priori*, but are derived from raw materials and industrial techniques. They even have an interchangeable potential (*Stoffwechseltheorie*), shown in the synthetic diagram presented in Figure 5.1.

Semper sees wood as the most architectonic material because of its potential to form articulated structures, illustrated through images of furniture and rooves (Semper, 1989). Thus, in Semper's theory of carpentry, rigid frames are analogous to flexible textile frames, which allows wooden constructions to easily incorporate decorative textile motifs. Consequently, the expressiveness of the art of tectonics is the result of external aesthetic references and the physical characteristics of its material (elasticity, flexibility, lightness, possibility of being cut in different formats) (Semper, 1989, pp.624-639). In summary, the connection between material and immaterial scales in Semper's theory of form refers to the phenomenon of expressivity as being intrinsic to techniques, like carpentry, as well as how certain techniques allow the architect to incorporate meaningful references and ornaments. In short, Semper's elements relate to aspects that are considered both functional and symbolic. The potential of Semper's argument, by recognizing that basic functions of a building are culturally symbolic, can be explored by any designer as a way of connecting material to immaterial scales. Semper further argues that the material is a key to understanding the artistic form, but it is not enough to create art forms. "Material only serves the idea; it is either better or less suited to this or that artistic purpose than another and is chosen accordingly without affecting the basic principles of art". (Semper, 1989, p.651). "[...] The material is only one of the determinants of art and architecture, but it is not the only one. The artist is therefore obliged to give emphasis to the material" Semper (1989, p.243)[2].

Figure 5.1 Tridimensional diagram summarizing Gottfried Semper's theory

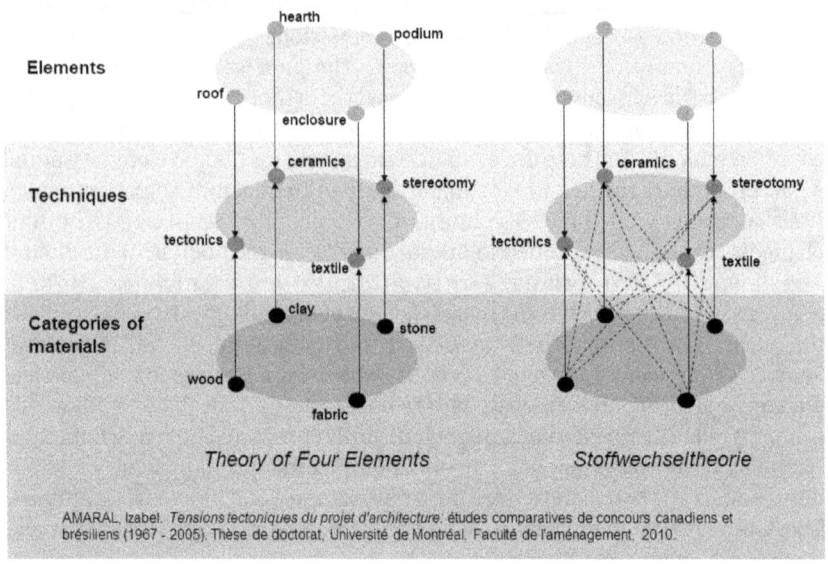

Notes:
- (left) the relationships between elements, techniques and materials; (right) the theory of material transformation (*Stoffwechseltheorie*),
- (right) the diagonal lines represent interchangeable possibilities between techniques and materials
- Adapted from: Amaral (2010) Most of the time, Semper's work has served to discuss the context of the design process, both for the architect and for artists, with an insistence on the aesthetic and symbolic relations between materials, forms and processes. A question that arises is this: is there validity in considering Semper's arguments as a means of thinking about sustainable architecture?

Although Semper is contemporary to the American pioneer of Environmentalism, George Perkins Marsh, *Der Stil*'s first edition appeared three years before Marsh's own *Man and Nature* (1864). Semper's search for the origins of ornaments can be compared to that of Charles Darwin in *Origins of Species*,

---

[2] This argument is also present in (Semper, 1984)

published a year before Semper's work (Mallgrave & Contandriopoulos, 2006, p.547). Contrary to Darwin's evolutionist hypothesis, however, Semper especially advocates an architecture that is consistent in the use of its materials and ornaments, without searching for searching to explain an evolutionary lineage of ornaments. Semper proclaims the existence of a cause-and-effect relationship between material and form: an ideal relationship which he justifies based on the technical origins of the ornaments. He insists throughout his discourse that architecture should be inspired by nature and its patterns, that it should observe how the natural environment deals with great varieties of species through an economy of strategies and forms, and that it should be integrated into the landscape. He gives the example of the Swiss house:

> "In fact, harmonizing with nature is architecture's only solution to being obliged to work within such overwhelming surroundings. For architecture to compete with nature, to set itself against nature effectively, is impossible. And yet here too contrasting effects can be discerned: the low squat proportions, the shallow roof, the warm colour, the comfortably cramped family quarters, all serving as a foreground for the noble but somewhat cold natural scene climbing towards the heavens" (Semper, 1989, pp.691-692).

No matter how memorable this argument may be, however, nature is evidently not a central notion in *Der Stil*, and it would be historically inappropriate to revisit Semper's work and look for critical perspectives on the drastic effects of industrialization. In the *Prolegomena* of *Der Stil*, Semper analyzes the three axes of formation through which plants and animals developed their formal attributes: symmetry, proportion and direction. He then describes how, by employing these axes in a variety of combinations, we can understand the forms of the natural world. Semper was interested in nature as a creative and formalistic principle. He once said: "Art, like nature, displays a similar variety of combinations but cannot exceed nature's bounds by an inch; its principles of formal configuration must be in strict accordance with the laws of nature" (Semper, 1989, p.92).

Nature represents an aesthetic paradigm for Semper, but it is not close to a contemporary symbolic logic of sustainable buildings, which reflect how "the new paradigm in the building arts is based on ecological models" (Guy & Farmer, 2000, p.79). Semper's theory of art and architecture has certainly much to contribute to sustainable building practices, and it addresses one of the missions of sustainable buildings: to "inspire and convey an increasing identification with Nature and the non-human world" Semper (1989, p.80).

German philosopher Gernot Böhme (2016) invoked one of Plato's dialogues on beauty, which addresses its relationship to the appropriateness of materiality. As he notes, the dichotomy of form and material runs parallel to the dichotomy of form and function, as first formulated by Plato. For the Greek philosopher, beauty is associated with the choice of the most appropriate material, thus reconciling form, material and function. Therefore, a golden ladle cannot be considered beautiful, but a fig ladle can "even make the soup smell better" (Böhme, 2016, p.49). Aesthetics, says Böhme, is related to the "sensual-affective attendance to things". This subject is, however, surprisingly intricate to economic conditions, as Böhme points out. There is a disconnect between delusion and imitation of materials, that dissociates an object's material from its actual appearance. For Böhme, the disconnect between exterior finishes and interiors, which are often economically derived, is ever more evident as one tries to make something look the same while simultaneously making it cost less.

Semper's work reminds us of the importance of materials, particularly raw materials, as a piece of the puzzle that is sustainability. Material can be one perspective from which to think about sustainability. It can also remind us that materials influence multiple scales: form, process and culture. What, though, are today's categories of raw materials? Can materials be idealized, as in Semper's theory?

From a sustainable perspective, there has been a shift in the understanding of *ideal materials*. Semper imagined four main categories of natural raw materials. Today, however, ideal materials can no longer be generalized and applied in a prescriptive manner. One must now consider transportation, energy efficiency, limiting the use of non-renewable resources, and alternatives to ecological systems of production, consumption and management of waste. Today's aesthetic perception of materials includes an appreciation of the process as much as any of the outcomes.

FRAMPTON'S THEORY OF TECTONICS: TOPOGRAPHY, PHENOMENOLOGY AND RESISTANCE

The end of the 19th century was an important phase for architectural theory. The discussions of materiality, characteristic of the works of Bötticher and Semper, made room for another theme that would come to play a central role in how architecture was theorized: the notion of space. Alongside with the notion of function, discussions on space eclipsed most of the debate about materiality during the 20th century. Yet, since the 1980s, tectonics has become one of the main topics of contemporary debate, together with semiotics, phenomenology, deconstructivism, and critical regionalism (Nesbitt, 1996).

Building up from the historical debate on tectonics, and strongly documented by a series of six case studies on Modern Architecture, Kenneth Frampton's contribution to the study of Modern Architecture builds on the historical debate concerning tectonics and represents a dive into an even more sophisticated interpretation of architecture, supporting itself with references to contemporary developments in phenomenology, semiotics and sociopolitical theory. More specifically, Frampton shows how modern architects have had in fact put into practice a refined approach to construction that addressed aesthetic, socioeconomic, and technical questions. Frampton's theory of tectonics posits that architecture comprises a so-called ontological dimension, corresponding to its physical manifestation, and a representational dimension, corresponding to the manifestation of a poetic leap. Thus, when architecture is in what the author calls the tectonic mode, the relations of the architectural form to its physical matter are so legitimate that the object will belong simultaneously to the technical sphere, as well as to a sensitive, symbolic and cultural sphere.

Many ideas bridge Semper and Frampton's arguments. For instance, there is the insistence on the phenomenon of being true to materials and place, which results in a *proclivity for the tactile*. Leaving aside any doctrinal tendencies, it is worth noting that Semper and Frampton's analyses of architecture ultimately take the form of theoretical statements on founding notions of the discipline. In the case of Semper, his evolutionary approach seeks virtue in myths of the primitive hut, the four elements of architecture, and the four technical arts. In the case of Frampton, the debate centres on contemporary issues, such as the relationship to the site, to the body, to perception, and to image and meaning, as well as ethnography. For both theorists, architectural craft represents a moral compromise between aesthetics and building matter. This moral compromise involves the relationship between material and form, but it also involves social ethics, as Frampton argues that good architecture should resist the forces of capitalism and the global process of commodification (Frampton, 1995, p.377).

From Semper to Frampton, the discourse on aesthetic perception has clearly shifted from a formalistic approach – which emphasizes the formal attributes of architecture – to considering the social role of experiences in aesthetic perception. The works of Gernot Böhme explain how the aesthetic experience relates not only to the body but to a sensual affective part of cultural experiences as well (Böhme, 2016).

The work of Dimitri Pikionis exemplifies for Frampton how topography is related to tectonics. The relation between building and site is mostly determined by the act of transformation and perception. Pikionis's promenade in Athens is more an act of collage than a design process, Frampton says, since its paving was done with leftover pieces of masonry and sculpture, thus showing no technological exhibitionism. The topographical dimension and the notion of the site relate to how the human body perceives both the natural and built environment. The very presence of a building on the ground is the first form of contact the human body makes the architecture, by means of the approach on the site (Frampton, 1995, pp.8-11). Edification alters the topographical dimension, evoking an expression that Frampton borrows from Vittorio Gregotti: the *architectural modification*, which is the inevitable encounter of the artificial with the natural. For Gregotti, a building influences the site in a reciprocal manner. Then, considering the cognitive process of metaphor, Frampton explains how one understands and structures his/her experiences and emphasizes how the body uses its tactile experience of reality to reconstruct the world. This is how architectural forms have a psychophysical impact on human beings. The many human perceptions of the architectural object may be "contrasting tactile experiences" in relation to light, smells, textures or different sensations related to closing, opening, etc. (Frampton, 1995, p.12). But how does one create and stimulate these tactile experiences? How does one train other architects to do the same?

The relation of architecture to the ground is fundamentally founded in the physics of construction. There is no building without groundwork. It is inevitable. In Le Corbusier's three "reminders to architects" (volume, surface, plan), the plan is a "generator of volume and surface," and the structure, he says, "rises from the base and develops according to a rule that is written on the ground in the plan" (Le Corbusier, 1924, p.9). The works of Semper, Bötticher and Frampton consider the footprint on the ground as a determining factor of architectural expression. The footprint includes dealing with the geographical conditions, accesses, orientation, footings and earthwork. We know that medieval cathedral builders used to trace plans, sections and drawings of architectural elements at a 1:1 plaster floors, a fact that reinforces Frampton's arguments. In fact, the plan was a generator of structure. As Robin Evans (2000, p.226) explains, for example, complex geometries drawn on the ground plan allowed builders to create sophisticated ribbed vaults in gothic cathedrals. Therefore, considering the relationship to the site and the concepts of Earthwork and Roofwork, tracing and span systems were a starting point for pedagogical experimentation related to tectonics and research-creation (Figure 5.2 and Figure 5.3 present examples of these pedagogical experimentations related to tectonics and research-creation).

Figure 5.2 First-year Studio assignment, study on the notions of Roofwork and Earthwork – 2018

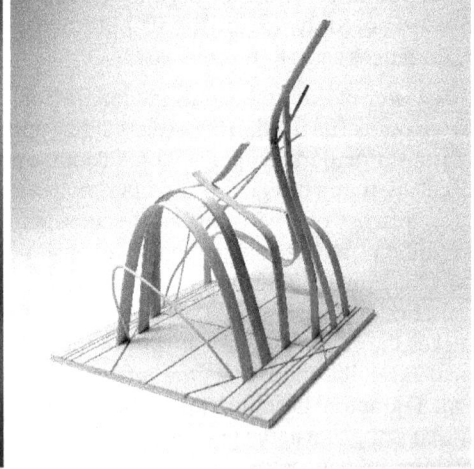

Notes:
- The assignment started by preparing the base of the model and creating slots, then limited to the slots, students would experiment building a roof structure with wood, floss and wire. Since glue or nails were not allowed, the models constitute more than representations, they are above all constructive experimentations of material, form and forces that teach about building from the ground-up.
- Student work, courtesy of Brook-Lynn Roy (left) and Sarah Chin (right)

Figure 5.3 The performance Dancing Geometry presented at the 3rd Nuit Blanche. Sudbury, Ontario - 2019

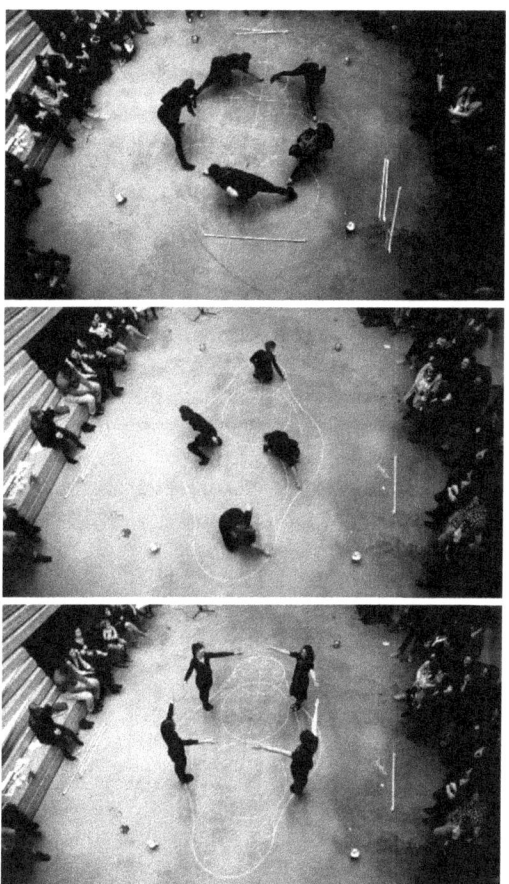

Notes:
- the floor was used as an extrapolation of drawings on paper, and as a generator of architectural forms.
- (left) an ornamented demonstration of Euclid's construction of a pentagon; (center and right) the plan at 1:3 scale of Borromini's San Carlo alle Quattro Fontane
- Performed by: Izabel Amaral, Kayla Korb, Cassidy Duff, Brianna Lafrenière, Sarah Tyler. Copyright Izabel Amaral

BRIDGING IMMATERIAL SENSE AND FORM-MAKING

In the existing, pluralistic discourse on the term tectonics, there resides a sign of healthy critical thinking about form, material, topography, nature, and perception that is crucial to sustainable design practices. For Semper, the connection of material to immaterial reflects on the expressivity of techniques, like the knot, that mobilize symbolic references through ornamentation. For Frampton (1995), a full representational dimension of architecture emerges from the encounter of the artificial with the natural, the building and the site, and a tactile bodily perception of the built world. These contributions convey core principles of sustainable design, which include moral judgments of beauty, such as being true to materials. It also includes considerations ranging from preoccupations to the body, the site and local cultures. These principles stand in accordance with the understanding of "sustainable design as the design of vibrant spaces and cultural places that makes environmental health an equally important condition" (Cucuzzella, 2015, p.88).

In Georg Willem Hegel's philosophy of the arts, architecture and poetry are situated at opposite poles, the first being the most material art and the second the most immaterial. Hegel's ideas have haunted architecture throughout history, thus architects have struggled to release buildings from their materiality, and tried to justify that architecture could be as intangible as poetry. The theory of tectonics tries to reconciliate Hegel's opposite poles through an esteem for materiality. Today, because of an insistence on the relevance of human experience of the built environment it should be an unquestionable component of sustainable design practices, even if it only addresses the topic of sustainability indirectly. The theory of tectonics, however, focuses mostly on visual and perceptive aspects of buildings, and even though Frampton considers a broad vision of human experience, discourse on tectonics relates to the perception of a final product. At present, we need to find alternative systems of production and ways of making through exemplary production processes, which can be explored in pedagogical situations.

In order to design sustainably, it is a matter of great importance that we at look how buildings can be impermanent, so as to represent a return to nature. Some design strategies focus on resource efficiency, limiting our consumption of material resources by directly restricting the amount of material used in buildings. Both building with a small number of light materials and optimizing the ratio of quality to weight are relevant strategies that designers can use to incorporate sustainable practices in their architectural forms. Other strategies may also include buildings that are thought to be disassembled, recycled and reused, as well as buildings addressing new methods for zero consumption, emission, or waste (Sobek, 2010, p.35). There are also concerns about which building techniques should be the most promoted. Due to recent developments in timber industries, wood technologies have been undeniably promoted as a means of realizing an environmentally sustainable world, with proponents citing their potential for carbon storage and efficiency as a renewable resource (Dangel, 2017). For this reason, revisiting the historical debate on tectonics is of greatest importance, since there are many fundamental principles related to wood buildings as being paradigmatic to architecture. One might expect that timber materials of today include traditional ways of building as well as recent engineered wood products, that call for a total new formal departure. Architectural education has to address both circumstances, the thinking of craft is relevant to creating meaningful architecture.

Stimulating craft and aesthetic may be a way of addressing new paradigm shifts in the discourse on sustainability, as Ruby and Ruby affirm, "the transition from a fossil to a post-fossil society allows us to embrace a more fruitful way to deal with surplus – the art of spending" (Ruby & Ruby, 2011, pp.15-16). Architectural education will take some time to reprogram itself. Considering Georges Bataille's radical critique of economy, society should spend their production surpluses through notions such as excess and expenditure instead of reinvestment in production, as in a traditional capitalist economy (Ruby & Ruby, 2011).

POETRY AS STRUCTURE: THE IMMATERIAL NATURE OF SUSTAINABLE TECTONICS

Design-build pedagogy presumes the transferability of learning from small-scale projects, pursued in an educational context, to larger-scale projects in professional practice. Material choices and building methods must be considered in the context of socio-cultural, environmental and economic sustainability. In addition to the design of a building, this pedagogy requires the design of other necessary processes associated with the building, and, most of the time, this practice takes longer than traditional studio projects (Stonorov, 2018).

In line with recent socially rooted practices in Canadian architecture, the creation of a new school of architecture in Northern Ontario was the subject of a long process that involved, among others, Laurentian University, the area's Francophone and Indigenous communities, and the citizens of the city of Sudbury. The product of a collaborative project, the McEwen School of Architecture, founded in 2013, included a design-build pedagogy intended to stimulate a dialogue with local industries and to function in accordance with the university's tri-cultural mandate bridging Anglophone, Francophone and Indigenous cultures. As a studio professor for first-year students, I teach a Francophone group. Every year, the studio participates in the project of an Ice Station, designed in the fall, built in the winter, and then placed on a lake in downtown Sudbury. Based on the idea that "architecture is not here to stay" (Sobek, 2010), Ice Stations are entirely made of wood and designed to be disassembled and recycled. As a pedagogical experience, it ties a hands-on experience to a *cradle-to-cradle* approach to buildings. The greatest challenge refers to a balance between a creative impulse and rational strategies for the reuse of wood. Even if the Ice Station experiment represents a small-scale design, it tackles important issues from design process and sustainable building strategies to the interpretation of a northern place[3].

In the context of a predominantly Anglophone milieu, the Ontarian Francophone minority is ingrained with a fatalistic attitude towards its own destiny, thus uprooting itself from its own cultural identity (Cazabon, 2007). For the group, the risk of linguistic assimilation is nuanced by its inclusion in a neo-Francophonie

---

[3] New coverage for the project was provided through CTV news: https://northernontario.ctvnews.ca/video?clipId=1896331

product of cultural diversity and globalization (Baudu, 2014). How does one design for such a context and how does one communicate to students that their design can have a positive influence on the local Francophone community?

Turning to literature, such as the work of dramaturge Jean-Marc Dalpé, one can find references to a *lieux de mémoire* and collective identity associated with place—the inhospitable landscape of Northern Ontario, in particular (Hotte, 2008). For Hotte (2008), Northern Ontario's French literature refers to common places, such as villages and houses, as if they were emblematic of the place. The poem *Gens d'ici* (1974), by Jean-Marc Dalpé, was read at the launch of the Ice Station project, and an excerpt from the text was inscribed inside the building itself. Both of these actions were taken as a means of engendering a stronger cultural understanding of the site and reconnecting Hegel's opposite poles of poetry and architecture.

Figure 5.4 The building activities for the Ice Station. Sudbury, Ontario - 2018.

Notes:
- (top) carving Dalpé's text, courtezy of Jonathan Kabumbe;
- (bottom left) production of modular pieces, (bottom right) assembly of structure, courtezy of Brook-Lynn Roy

Connections of immaterial 111

Wood was the only material used in the project it did not employ fasteners and glue, hinting at the designers' goal of producing a building that was non-toxic and biodegradable. This approach to construction was made possible by a reconceptualization of joinery as structural articulation, come-upon by the designers while researching traditional assembly techniques. The team behind the building wished to optimize its modular components and make construction as quickly as possible. As a result, part of the structure was made using industrial manufacture strategies. Dalpé's poem, however, was being carved by hand, complicating this somewhat.

During the building's four weeks of construction, two teams were working simultaneously: the first producing the modular pieces and a second carving Dalpé's text (process seen in Figure 5.4). Each letter could take up to 30 minutes. The teams would swap roles at regular intervals, allowing students to learn about every step of the construction process. After discussing how their project would be received by non-French speakers, the group made the decision to translate key words of Dalpé's work into English and Ojibway and include them on benches surrounding the building. The poem's main text is engraved on horizontal planks that give lateral stability to the pavilion and hold all of its components together. Without the planks, the entire structure would collapse like a spring, and each ring would fall outward. Because the structure was one single entity, this also meant that it was impossible to assemble its parts separately and then transport them to the site. The poetry provided structure its architecture on both a literal and metaphorical level. As in Semper's example of the knot as an artistic symbol, lengths of sisal rope were used to literally sew the poem to the pavilion, reinforcing the idea that the building conveyed symbolic meaning.

Figure 5.5 Ice Station's structural details. Sudbury, Ontario - 2018

Notes:
- Construction without fasteners or glue. Author's photo.

Figure 5.6 Ice Station constructed and in its context. Sudbury, Ontario – 2018. Author's photo.

The Ice Station acts as an example of how, when building with biodegradability in mind, one needs to improve the level of craft and dedicate as much attention to the process as to the final product. Slow processes, like engraving, allow for deep appreciation of materials, deep learning of skills, and an efficient use of a given workforce, all ultimately in accordance with a style of craft that does not aim at rapid production. Considering that wooden architecture is presumed to be a key component of the architectural fight against climate change, preparing architecture students to be knowledgeable about working with the material becomes increasingly important with each passing day. For instance, the Ice Station project shows that traditional wood assemblies are capable of taking on a great number of forms, a fact that confirms Gottfried Semper's theory about the

Connections of immaterial

potential of the material in exemplary architecture (details of the structure and its assembly are seen in Figure 5.5).

Figure 5.7 Details of Jean-Marc Dalpé's engraved poem on the Ice Station's horizontal boards. Sudbury, Ontario – 2018. Author's photo

Pragmatic solutions can be viewed as active nourishment to the poetic side of the architectural project. For architecture students, knowledge of structural principles and a rational understanding of fabrication methods can condense lessons that will later be incorporated in larger-scale projects. These principles are necessarily important to sustainable building practices, since they allow for buildings to adapt quickly to changing needs and architects to develop more critical perspectives on ethics and authenticity. Rational, modular building systems are able to assume different functions over time. This is a desirable quality for sustainable buildings, as it prolongs their life spans, reduces their environmental footprints, and promotes long-term social acceptance. Additionally, structural modularity and simplicity may be key to addressing sustainable design potentially even becoming means of portraying buildings in a positive, eco-friendly light. The craft involved in a building's detail unquestionably influences aesthetic appreciation and promotes a sense of community. Images of the final constructed project and its details are presented in Figure 5.6 and the engraved poem in Figure 5.7.

Sudbury's Ice Station project puts forth a rigorous means of connecting the technical (material) and symbolic (immaterial) dimensions of architecture. The representational dimension of a building may relate to a symbolic reference, which may consequently include fewer concerns about the material presence of the work. This materiality is not a priority of the designer, but rather part of a symbolic reference that will engage the public. In this case, the target of the design process is not the object itself, but its public reception. When the material dimension is not related to the material dimension, the result ends up being something of a banal *decorated warehouse*, conveying an obvious message meant for quick, easy consumption. Such architecture was at the centre of the critiques by theorists like Semper and Frampton. In short, only when a project demonstrates a search for balance between the technical and symbolic dimensions, should it be considered consistent with the concept of sustainable tectonics, respecting the rules of a moral compromise with land, material, and humanity.

CONCLUSION

The aesthetics of sustainable buildings are a mediated experience, made possible by knowledge, both subjective and objective, about the durable and environmental aspects of building elements. For instance, using raw, naturally-sourced materials, as in Semper's theory, allows for their easy appreciation. Our pedagogical experience shows that, if one wishes to make a fully biodegradable building, especially one constructed from wood, the use of a minimal palette of materials that such a project entails will require highly elaborate craftmanship to succeed. This has an influence on users' subjective experience and on their visual and tactile appreciation of craft. The nature of the moral compromise with material has, recently, been experiencing a significant transformation. It has begun moving from a formalistic, technical and pragmatic understanding of material properties to a cultural-symbolic one. If we wish to ensure that human diversity enjoys a long lifespan, however, we must include a diversity of ethical perspectives in this new understanding as soon as possible.

REFERENCES

Amaral, I. (2010). *Tensions tectoniques du projet d'architecture: études comparatives de concours canadiens et brésiliens (1967-2005)*. Université de Montréal.

Baudu, L. J. (2014). *Les Canadiens francophones*. HD, Ateliers Henry Dougier.

Beim, A., & Stylsvig Madsen, U. (2014). *Towards an Ecology of Tectonics: The Need for Rethinking Construction in Architecture*. Edition Axel Menges.

Böhme, G. (2016). Material splendour: a contribution to the critique of aesthetic economy. In S. K. Löschke (Ed.), *Materiality and architecture* (pp. 47–58). Routledge, Taylor & Francis Group.

Bötticher, C. (1992). The Principles of Hellenic and Germanic ways of building. In W. Herrmann (Ed.), *In what style should we build? The German debate on architectural style* (pp. 147–167). Getty Center for the History of Art and the Humanities (Distributed by the University of Chicago Press).

Bötticher, K. G. W. (1852). *Die Tektonik der Hellenen* (W. Hermann (Ed.)). Ernst & Korn.

Cazabon, B. (2007). *Langue et culture: unité et discordance*. Prise de parole.

Chupin, J-P., & Simonnet, C. (Eds.). (2005a). *Le projet tectonique*. Infolio.

Chupin, J-P., & Simonnet, C. (2005b). Objets et trajets du projet tectonique. In J.-P. Chupin & C. Simonnet (Eds.), *Le projet tectonique* (pp. 7–13). Infolio.

Cucuzzella, C. (2015). Is Sustainability Reorienting the Visual Expression of Architecture? *RACAR: Revue d'art Canadienne, 40*(2), 86. https://doi.org/10.7202/1035398ar

Dangel, U. (2017). *Turning point in timber construction: a new economy*. Birkhauser.

Emmons, P. (2015). Architectural Encounters between Material and Idea. In M. Mindrup (Ed.), *The material imagination: reveries on architecture and matter* (pp. 89–106). Ashgate.

Evans, R. (2000). *The projective cast architecture: and its three geometries*. MIT Press.

Frampton, K. (1995). *Studies in tectonic culture: the poetics of construction in nineteenth and twentieth century architecture*. MIT Press.

Gottfried, S. (1860 – 1863). *Der Stil in den technischen und tektonischen Künsten, oder, Praktische Aesthetik: ein Handbuch für Techniker, Künstler und Kunstfreund* (2 volumes). Verlag für Kunst und Wissenschaft, Bruckmann's.

Guy, S., & Farmer, G. (2000). Contested Constructions: The competing logics of green buildings and ethics. In W. Fox (Ed.), *Ethics and The Built Environment* (pp. 73–87). Routledge.

Hale, J. A. (2000). *Building ideas: an introduction to architectural theory*. J. Wiley & Sons.

Herrmann, W. (1992). Introduction. In H. Hübsch et al, *In what style should we build? The German debate on architectural style.* (pp. 1-62). Getty Center for the History of Art and the Humanities (Distributed by the University of Chicago Press).

Hotte, L. (2008). Entre l'esthétique et l'identité: la création en contexte minoritaire. In J. Y. Thériault, A. Gilbert, & L. Cardinal (Eds.), *L'espace francophone en milieu minoritaire au Canada: Nouveaux enjeux, nouvelles mobilisations*. Fides.

Le Corbusier. (1924). *Vers une architecture*. Flammarion.
Löschke, S. K. (Ed.). (2016). *Materiality and architecture*. Routledge.
Mallgrave, H. F. (1983). *The Idea of Style: Gottfried Semper in London*. University of Pennsylvania.
Mallgrave, H. F., & Contandriopoulos, C. (2006). *Architectural Theory, Vol 1: An Anthology from Vitruvius to 1870* (H. F. Mallgrave & C. Contandriopoulos (Eds.). Blackwell Publishing.
Marsh, G. P. (1864). *Man and nature*. Belknap Press of Harvard University Press.
Nesbitt, K. (1996). Introduction. In K. Nesbitt (Ed.), *Theorizing a New Agenda for Architecture - An Anthology of Architectural Theory 1965-1995* (pp. 16–70). Princeton Architectural Press.
Ruby, I., & Ruby, A. (Eds.). (2011). *Re-inventing Construction*. Ruby Press.
Schwarzer, M. (1993). Ontology and Representation in Karl Bötticher's Theory of Tectonics. *Journal of the Society of Architectural Historians, 52*(3), 267–280.
Schwarzer, M. (1998). Karl Gottlieb Wilhelm Bötticher. In *Encyclopedia of Aesthetics* (p. 291). Oxford University Press.
Semper, G. (1984). Attributes of Formal Beauty (1856-59). In W. Herrmann (Ed.), *Gottfried Semper: in search of architecture* (pp. 219–224). MIT Press.
Semper, G. (1989). *The four elements of architecture and other writings* (H. F. Mallgrave & W. Herrmann (Trans.)). Cambridge University Press.
Semper, G. (2004). *Style in the technical and tectonic arts, or, Practical aesthetics* (H. F. Mallgrave & M. Robinson (Trans.)). Getty Research Institute.
Sobek, W. (2010). Architecture Isn't Here to Stay: Toward a Reversibility of Construction. In I. Ruby & A. Ruby (Eds.), *Re-inventing Construction* (pp. 34–45). Ruby Press.
Stonorov, T. (2018). *The Design-build studio: crafting meaningful work in architecture education*. Routledge.

CHAPTER 6

EDITORS' PREFACE

Ted Cavanagh's essay complements Amaral's view on the importance of making in sustainable architecture. He proposes to study sustainable architecture practices across a grid comprised of two polarities: the global vs. local, on one hand, and tailored vs. replicable on the other. He uses the grid to explore theories and practices relating to appropriate and prototyping technologies. To decipher some of those tensions, Cavanagh studies a built project aligned with the theory and practice of proper design and compares it with a built project that, intentionally, explores the theory and practice of prototyping. By drawing on the distinction between types of appropriate and prototypical technologies, the essay highlights the locality embedded in the first. He highlights the danger of convoluting the definition of appropriate technologies with environmentally sound technologies (which he remarks on the international scale); a confusion that can disembody the local character of appropriate technology. From a sustainable architecture perspective, the questions of locality, appropriateness and community are being replaced with environmentally focused approaches that promise improvements in building components and yet fail to address whole building-level concerns.

Intentions and Consequences: Prototyping and Appropriate Technology

Ted Cavanagh

Dalhousie University

INTRODUCTION

"The first step in developing a politics of techno-science is to think our way out of any historicist determinism or imagined necessity regarding the technological. There is no neat line of modes of production; there is only the conflictual development of technologies. And the exposure of this history opens up a way, both to resist the dominant techno-logic of the First World and, to avoid the romanticism of the non- or less-technological other worlds. On a practical level, artists, critics, and architects might articulate the contradictions between our given techno-social paradigms ... Once exposed, these contradictions might renew a whole range of positions, each for a specific context or conjuncture. Such a revision might even allow for 'convivial' uses of the technological and – who knows – maybe even utopian uses" (Foster, 1987, p.63)[1].

In the creative fields, the relationship between theory and practice is not always clear (Jorgensen, 2005). Architecture's local and global scales, too, give rise to further ambiguity. On one hand, the discipline is immobile, and sustainable practices of building are dependent on local labour and materials. On the other hand, technology is mobile, and advances in sustainable practices are occurring worldwide. In order to discuss local and global scales of sustainability, this chapter studies a built project aligned with the theory and practice of appropriate design and compares it with a built project that intentionally explores the theory and practice of prototyping.

It is likely that theory and practice are separate but parallel projects in a body of work. Different projects by the same architect can draw on different theoretical assumptions and practical strategies, just as they can have different premises. Thus, a body of work can be differentiated into distinctive projects of theory and of

---

[1] Quote from: the "Concluding Notes" on page 63 of *Building, Machines* published by the Princeton Architectural Press – book editor is McCarter, Robert. This publication was the 12th volume in the Pamphlet Architecture series.

Intentions and Consequences 119

practice. This chapter compares two projects in practice and associates them with two different theories; the fact that this a retrospective view makes analysis easier.

My body of work includes two projects that were designed and built in 2004 and 2014 for the same client. The projects shared the same location and were similar in size. The outdoor children's theatre, Le Petit Cercle (Figure 6.1), was a simple composition of locally sourced materials; whereas, the market, Le Marché Fermier (Figure 6.2), incorporated global technology and sophisticated design. Each building used bentwood components in different ways. The theatre used lumber from a local lumber yard that had been left outside during the rainy summer, as such it was cheap and easy to bend. The amount of strain the lumber would tolerate was gauged by walking it into curves and sensing when it was about to break, then backing off a bit. All connections were conventional, done with standard deck screws and carpenter glue. Models and mock-ups were assessed visually to verify constructability.

Figure 6.1 Le Petit Cercle, Children's Theatre – 2004

Notes:
- Designed and built in two weeks by Ted Cavanagh, Richard Kroeker, Roger Mullin, Alden Neufeld and 23 students of the Dalhousie School of Architecture.
- Overall dimensions: 180 seats, 12 foot by 20-foot stage, an overall length of 75 feet, and an overall width 30 feet.
- Walls: 16-foot vertical ribs laminated one by fours on wood blocking, diagonal one-by-three spruce each side screwed to ribs, rock infill for ballast.
- Floor: smooth gravel six inches deep.

- Stage: one-by-four floor deck on one-by-tens with suspended rock infill.
- Seats: recycled bleachers and new lumber.
- Other: Playground slide doubles as an entry. Long axis oriented southeast to head into prevailing winds.

Figure 6.2 Marché Fermier, Farmers' Market – 2014

Notes:
- Designed and built in eight months by Ted Cavanagh and 14 students of the Dalhousie School of Architecture.[2]
- Overall dimensions: 20 market stalls, an overall length of 75 feet, and an overall width of 20 feet.
- Walls: poured concrete, curved, west wall 18 inches high, east wall 36 inches high
- Roof: red oak (green state), polyuthethane glue at scarf joints, steel connections at walls
- Floor: poured concrete slab.
- Stage: two-by-three floor deck on two-by-eights.
- Stalls: new dimension lumber.

In the market, the size of the wood was determined by the engineers. However, little was known about wood's behaviour when bent. We tested different cross sections and wood species in our laboratory. Our selection, 60 mm wide red oak, was sourced at a regional wood lot and custom sawn into 20 mm thicknesses. Models were cast in plaster, and others were made with structural software. These were carefully assessed and translated into design information. Design and construction were separate phases and included an intermediate stage of design development using trial installations, mock-ups and on-site structural tests (Figure 6.3). Thus, the material of the two projects can be compared at the level of the connection, the building, and the various domains (retail, wholesale, production, and government),

---

[2] The Marché Fermier, Farmers' Market is the first of a series of four gridshell buildings built between 2014 and 2018 in Louisiana, Arizona and Nova Scotia. A social and technological analysis of the gridshell series is found in Verderber, S., Cavanagh, T. & Oak, A. (2019). *Thinking While Doing: Explorations in Educational Design/Build*. Birkhauser.

Intentions and Consequences 121

as well as through the use of scaling as part of the process of design.[3&4] Simply put, these two projects are sustainable in different but comparable ways.

Figure 6.3 Design and construction experimentation for the two featured projects

---

[3] For a discussion of the concept of domains see Cowan, R. (1985). The Consumption Junction: A Proposal for Research Strategies in the Sociology of Technology. In W. Bijker, T. Hughes, & T. Pinch (Eds.), *The Social Construction of Technological Systems* (pp. 262–280). MIT Press.
[4] For a discussion of scaling as part of the design process see Yaneva, A. (2005). Scaling Up and Down: Extraction Trials in Architectural Design. *Social Studies of Science*, *35*(6), 867–894. https://doi.org/10.1177/0306312705053053

Chapter 6

COMPARING THEORIES, COMPARING PROJECTS

This chapter focuses on two theoretical concepts – prototyping (PT) and appropriate technology (AT) – as developed in the literature of design studies and technology studies. PT and AT have a field of positions between them. Locating projects in this field is a form of critical measurement. Here, the field is visualized as a domain where various issues have co-ordinates of location. The intent is to create a map for critical clarification without a claim of precision – seen in Figure 6.4.

Figure 6.4 A map for critical clarification between prototyping and appropriate technology – focusing on the factors of the two featured projects

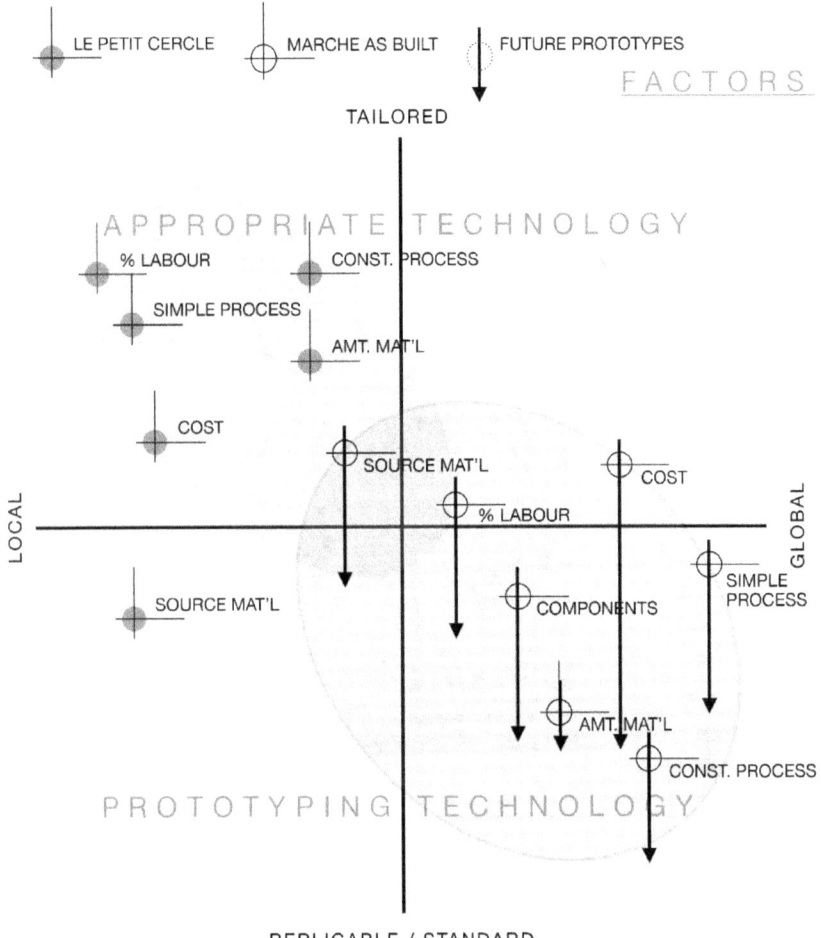

In most common usage, PT would emphasize the global, while AT would emphasize the local. The local/global distinction forms the x-axis in Figure 6.4. As Guy and Farmer (2001) have shown, there are many ways of building sustainably, and the place is definitely a factor. Localness cannot presume place. Rather, there is a critical measure of the degree of fit, achieved through idiosyncrasy or tailoring. Internationality implies not any single place in a utopian sense, but rather any place and common humanity. Global fit involves standardization and finding things in common. Thus, fit is measured along the y-axis, ranging from the custom and the tailored to the (new) standard and the universal.

In his review of the recent history of AT, Dean Nieusma (2004) describes the technology transfer trope of modernization for the 'Third World.' The concept of AT counters this trope through both radical, pro-autonomous and sustainable, low-impact technology[5]. As well, the term is generally understood to encompass technology that is small-scale, people-centred, decentralized, and locally autonomous[6]. In Nieusma's history, it was first manifest as universal design. Since then, "participatory design, ecological design, feminist design, and socially responsible design have gained various degrees of legitimacy in their efforts to design for marginalized groups" (Nieusma, 2004). AT gains acolytes as a political resistance to market and hegemonic forces and, in practice, bends technology toward a project's context and local perspectives.

This chapter compares and contrasts AT with an open-ended concept of PT drawn from several theoretical discussions.[7] PT emphasises a future-oriented investigation of the new. A number of authors see the technical as 'the kind of research that is carried out to explore possible worlds,' opening up territory through 'prototyping' and 'trail blazing' (Binder et al., 2015; Callon et al., 2009)[8]. The term 'prototype' is applicable to all stages of architectural production, from drawing [or drawing out] to building and further on to using (Hill, 2010). More important, from a comparative point of view, is the distinction made by those

---

[5] AT adapts to best fit the community in which it is developed because it is created by the people to meet a need. The concept stemmed from the work of British economist Dr. Fritz Schumacher. Schumacher, E.F. *Small is Beautiful: A Study of Economics as if People Mattered*. London: Dlond & Briggs Ltd, 1973. AT advocates put forward values under the rubric of social justice ranging from financial independence to environmental stewardship to political autonomy. 'Radical technology' sees the tools of technology and design as liberating techniques, sources of energy and as part of a restructured social order.

[6] Appropriate technology. Retrieved September 20, 2018, from https://en.wikipedia.org/wiki/Appropriate_technology. *Referencing OECD.* "Appropriate Technology". *Glossary of Statistical Terms*. Retrieved 24 April 2011

[7] The concepts of PT are summarised in theme issues of the *Journal of Cultural Economy* edited by Alberto Corsín Jiménez (including Guggenheim, 2014) and *Visual Communication* edited by Graeme Were (2010).

[8] Prototype does not mean "first of a type" in the sense of Laugier's primitive hut.

interested in PT between two kinds of democracy—deliberative and dialogic. The former is designed to aggregate people in forming the general will, and the latter is designed to promote collaborative research, and so to explore new identities and worlds (Jasanoff, 2012). PT aspires to a political re-inscription of democracy into things, and, in practice, it bends technology toward a project's broad impact and addition to knowledge.

Locality

The town was officially founded by Acadians returning a generation after their 1755 expulsion by the British. Their deportation to Louisiana and other French colonies is described by Longfellow in his epic poem Evangeline. In Chéticamp, stories are told of Acadians avoiding deportation by living inland out of sight of the British navy – land the British assumed was unsettled by the British because of the extreme wind. Over time, the French-speaking community developed a fishing economy and a way of dealing with the windy landscape.

Chéticamp is a port for the crab fishery and harbours a strongly local economy based on cooperatives; there are no national chain businesses, unusual for a town of three thousand. The long-lot land division creates a linear town and allows every resident ocean frontage. Everyone lives on the town's main street; a two-lane coastal highway called the Cabot Trail that attracts a quarter-million tourists each year. Chéticamp is a five-hour drive from Dalhousie in Halifax.

Any place where amazing winds blow, locals tend to give them a unique name. In Chéticamp, the winter and springtime southeasters are called *Suettes*. As often as five times a month, they reach speeds of 200 kilometers an hour. They speed down off the plateau and whip across the old playground behind the school. All shingles in the town are battened down, double nailed and tightly overlapped. Trucks with semi-trailers stop traveling on the roads.

Chéticamp is a unique locality. Its ways of building reflect a unique culture adapted to an extreme climate. The working vernacular, and even some of the domestic vernacular, reflect this context[9]. Clearly, AT would be influenced by the locale.

Project delivery

Since the mid-1980s, the Dalhousie School of Architecture has developed a culture of making. This all started with a six-week second-year design studio where

---

[9] Working and domestic vernacular refer to the occupancy of buildings and the use of objects, the former as part of local industry such as fishing or car mechanics and the latter is residential. Global influence is more pervasive in the domestic realm, whereas bricolage and local use of materials tend to be part of the day to day work world.

students built an architectural building fragment and related it to a 1:20 scale design model of the entire building. Starting in 1991, FreeLabs were introduced. These continue today. Every student goes through a two-week design/build studio, once as an undergraduate and once as a graduate (Macy, 2008). This process has cemented design and build culture as a core value in the curriculum. The FreeLabs have generated 250 projects during their twenty-five-year history. Notable among the projects have been the 2004 collaboration by three faculty for a children's theatre that won national and international awards and the Ghost Laboratory that has been extensively written on (Cavanagh et al., 2005; MacKay-Lyons & Buchanan, 2008).

Over the last ten years, Coastal Studio has completed several innovative structures designed to shelter community activities. Primarily, it does funded research into new ways of building, teaching students the ins and outs of innovation. The successful building prototypes are donated to communities for their use. Two early projects stand out, a wood lamella barrel vault and thin brick catenary shell. Early twentieth-century architects, Haring and Gaudi, worked with these construction techniques (Adriaenssens et al., 2014; Blundell-Jones, 2002). We utilized these techniques, updating them with advances from recent research and built projects. We pushed the technology by making our structures thinner and lighter and by building them in a northern climate (Cavanagh, 2013).

Coastal Studio is developing a rigorous way of working in design/build. Collaboration with other university design/build programs has made comparative analysis of methodology possible. Recently, each project has begun being recorded and analyzed by sociologists, anthropologists, historians, and philosophers. Each group tests the technological and social aspects of innovation for a contemporary advancement of construction techniques.

Our version of design build is a controlled experiment meant to create a prototype building in which the current application of a structural system is tested and extended. In the process of its realization, the building is conceptualized through a process of mocking up or prototyping the various details repeated throughout the final work.

LE PETIT CERCLE - 2004

Every July, instructors in our school guide students through a short design/build project. In 2004, a group of three instructors combined forces to construct a permanent building – an outdoor children's theatre suitable for the festival and a future theatre camp. On day one, we had a surrealistic derelict playground on a twelve-foot-high plateau behind the school, two thousand dollars and twenty-seven of us ready to design, build and raise money for the theatre. On day fifteen, we had a theatre designed, built and nearly paid for.

In 2004, the town hosted Le Troisième Congrès Mondiale Acadien, celebrating 400 years of European settlement in Canada. Festivities were organized in support of one hundred family reunions throughout the province. In Chéticamp, the church and the adjacent school contained three indoor spaces suitable for festival performances. Organizers added some temporary outdoor sites and talked optimistically of a permanent summer theatre camp in the old playground behind the school.

We started on day one with no predetermined design and presented a number of options to the local school and theatre group. Based on their feedback, we developed two hypothetical theatres – one that could be disassembled and hinged down for winter storage and permanent one that was *transparent to the wind*, heavy, yet perforated to reduce extreme wind load. In the winter, fishing boats were hauled up on land and cradled on simple structures using impossibly thin bent wood supports that supported the boats and their winter wind loads. Local wharves were constructed with wood cribs containing rock ballast. This cultural reinforcement persuaded us to build using rock-ballasted wooden cribwork for the walls and to create a permanent theatre using thin bentwood with minimal wind resistance – seen in Figure 6.5.

Figure 6.5 Wood cribs containing rock ballast in "Le Petit Cercle" - 2004

Intentions and Consequences 127

This method of design development surprised the students. Studio projects had not prepared them to elaborate options for the client nor to develop a number of design strategies in parallel. By day five, they no longer suspected that the instructors had prepared a secret design in advance; and, more importantly, they realized that the developing designs would be considered in terms of building performance evaluated by experiment and experience. From that point forward, the students became designer-builders, sorting out details and working on sub-projects nested within the developing design framework (the building process is illustrated in Figure 6.6).

Figure 6.6 The creation of "Le Petit Cercle", showing the crib work and curvature - 2004

This framework evolved based on a set of pragmatic and aesthetic considerations. For example, it was important to ballast the built structure; so, the mass was added low, suspended from the structure to avoid touching the ground. In another example, the siting of the theatre was the subject of some debate. Explorations of the slide revealed a huge concrete foundation. Plans to bring the slide to the theatre were discarded in favour of keeping it where it was, and the theatre was located around it (seen in Figure 6.7). The rain that filled the excavation became a means of leveling the site. The crib work became its own scaffolding. The curvature in the plan was based on the maximum the one-by-threes would tolerate. Luckily, they were still fairly green.

The amazingly short ten-day building period generated real excitement in the community and a strength of purpose in the architect/builders. There was a sense of ownership by all. The indications of the project's success are based in the architecture, but also based in the fact that it is a children's theatre, located in a unique French-speaking town and part of a very significant festival. The theatre company was impressed by the acoustics and the way the building tempered the climate. They planned night-time musical shows and imagined various lighting effects. Many qualities of the theatre were the product of design decisions that were synchronized by the immediacy of construction; there are many advantages to a compressed time scale. The reflection of Acadian culture was quick, compressed to the local scale in ways that were immediate, analogous and poetic. The mediation of climate drew inspiration from a survey of many local building details. At this scale, the strategies of resilience were simple and apparent, enabling adoption and adaptation at the detail and building scales.

Figure 6.7 Negotiating the location of "Le Petit Cercle" on the site in reference to the existing slide - 2004

LE MARCHÉ FERMIER - 2014

The structural form of the project, a vault, was a prerequisite, as was the grid shell structural system. During the first weeks of the studio, ten students investigated the overall form of the building, the node connection, and the lath material (the node connection is seen in Figure 6.8). They chose red oak and visited the local saw-mill to understand its selection and the milling process. The Spanish windlass was identified as a type of lashing worth investigating for performance and ease of construction. The overall form curved in plan, introducing significant double curvature in the vault (seen in Figure 6.9). As in our previous projects, the structure was intended to be open at each end. These openings faced away from the 200 kph winds. As a result, the convex side of the building pointed into and shed the wind. In the theatre built ten years before in Chéticamp, we had learned to let the wind through our building. In this case, the cells up to eye level would be free of permanent cladding and totally open during the winter suette season.

Intentions and Consequences

Figure 6.8 The 'noded-out' base connection of "Le Marché Fermier"- 2014

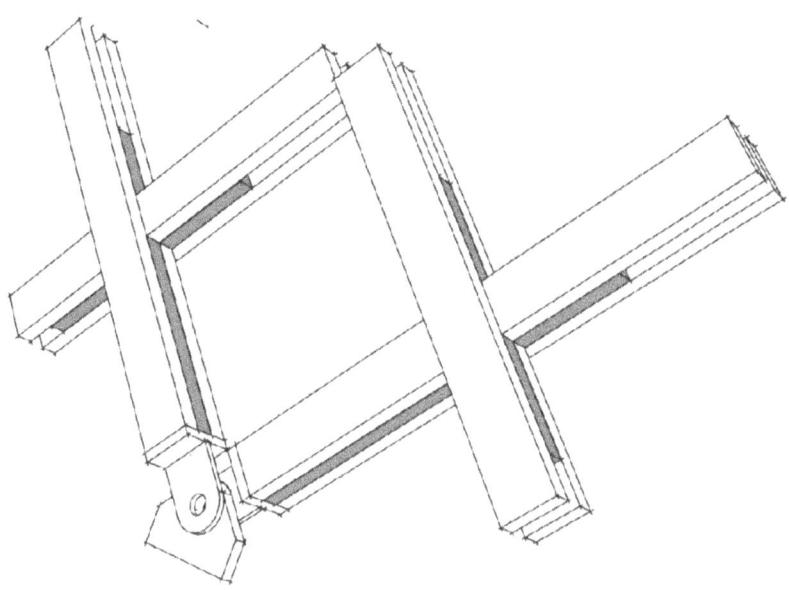

Figure 6.9 The double curvature in the plan of "Le Marché Fermier"- 2014

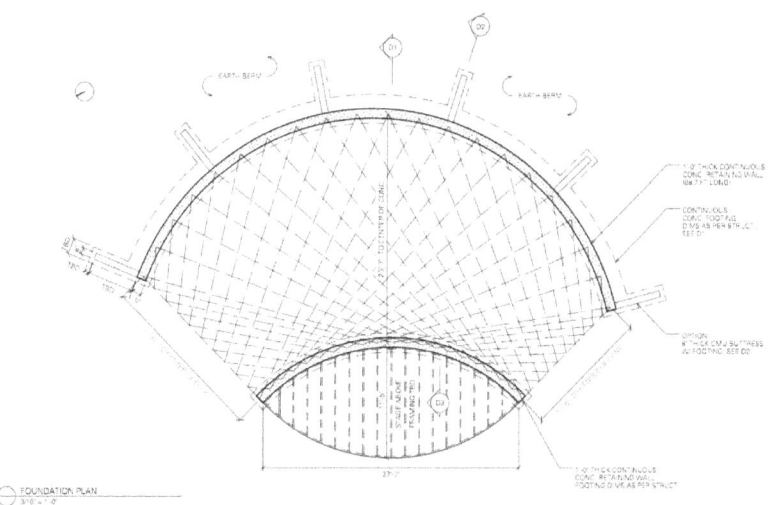

The supporting walls for the shell remained low so that it could come close to the ground. The land fell towards the harbour and away from the wind. The leeward walls were exposed and a half meter high, and the windward walls retained about a meter of earth. This had the effect of hunkering the building down and exposing less surface to the wind. The concave side created a natural shelter for a stage facing the harbour and the road. Raising the earth in a small berm that reflected the curvature in the shell's plan created an enclosing effect and a place for an audience to sit.

The student proposal formed the basis of consultation with the occupants and the client. Coastal Studio looks for opinions and suggestions, much like a conventional architectural practice. The occupants had concerns that the building was too small for the number of vendors, but in the end, they agreed to replace their huge tables with more compact market stalls. In addition, we made certain the occupants and the client understood the nature of our projects as building innovation research. Unlike practice, the projects are experiments in construction technique that could fail technically or be unrealizable.

Lawrence Friesen of Nomad Design Workshop in London took us through the first steps and principles of grid shell design. His explanation involved a compelling, iterative process between physical and digital models. It is argued that the purest type of grid shell is built flat, then sprung into its final form by restraining the perimeter to the designed plan (Chilton & Tang, 2017).

Figure 6.10 Physical model for "Le Marché Fermier" - 2014

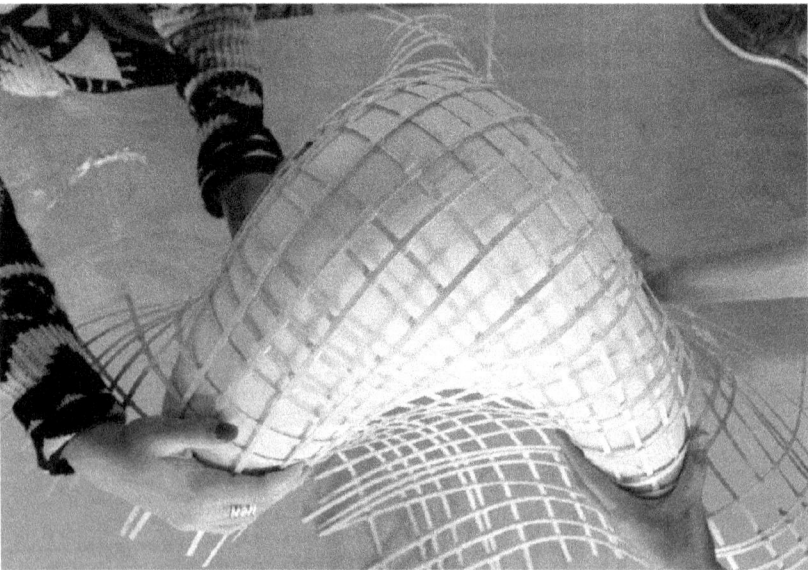

The first step simulated this pure type in a physical model (seen in Figure 6.10). Various plans were cut into a flat piece of wood, stretchable fabric was attached

Intentions and Consequences 131

around the plan perimeter, and plaster was poured into it. This approximated the spring of the shell from a restrained perimeter. It was an exercise in close reading and intense observation. It involved figuring out what the material was doing and why it was doing it. It was interpretive; a fold in the fabric mold under the weight of the plaster marked a spot where some of the surface needed to be removed in the next model. The various models were also compared for differences. For instance, the physical models correctly predicted that the open gable ends induced reverse curvature in the shell nearby and the structural and computer models did not (digital model seen in Figure 6.11).

Figure 6.11 Digital model for "Le Marché Fermier" - 2014

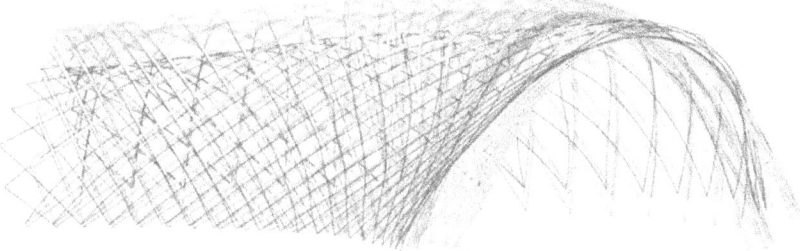

Figure 6.12 "Le Marché Fermier" in place - 2014

Once the form and plan were determined, the next step involved approximating the surface with a grid that represented the long strips of wooden lath. In the physical model, a grid was created on top of a pattern on the fabric form laid out flat. This was repeated in the computer model using a three-dimensional scan of the plaster model, laying the surface out flat and plotting linear members of the grid shell. Again, the models were observed closely. The perimeter condition of the linear grid determined whether it was going to 'node out.' This is a condition where every lath ends at the perimeter in tandem with the end of another lath going in the opposite direction, thus describing the perimeter as a series of nodes. In order to node out, the grid created a condition where the base connections would not be in a horizontal line, nor would they be in a uniform arch front and back. Obviously, some further constraints were necessary.

Figure 6.13 "Le Marché Fermier" in use - 2014

A number of directions were possible at this point in the design. Returning to the concept of the simple base attachment that noded out, we added three constraints. The connection points at the base were defined as nodes. Additionally, front and back curved walls were level on top and divided into an equal number of divisions. Further, the centre front was connected to each end of the back. The next step was to plot the laths as geodesics on the scanned surface of the plaster model. In design-build studios, assumptions must be made for the project to move forward; we only had six weeks left until completion.

Intentions and Consequences

The studio was twelve weeks long. During weeks five and six, we traveled to the Southeastern United States to visit other small buildings in fragile coastal landscapes, many design/build projects among them. The visit included the work of Mississippi State, Auburn, Tulane, Houston, Texas at Austin and at San Antonio. We viewed a project by Louisiana at Lafayette, as well and returned for week seven to build a 1:2 model of the structure on the front lawn of the school.

After twelve weeks, the shell was sprung, and the nodes and perimeter bolts were holding the structure in place. It was a satisfactory end to the studio, but it was obvious that substantial adjustments were needed before everything was locked in place (seen in Figure 6.12).

It is now five years later. The structure has withstood 250 km/hour winter storms with only minor damage to the cladding. Other grid shells have been built, and the farmers' market grid shell itself has become an example for others to learn from. Figure 6.13 shows the market in use.

APPROPRIATE TECHNOLOGY

Comparing these two projects brings up both similarities and differences. Two theories, or perhaps categorizations, can help structure this discussion. The children's theatre does not exactly match the principles of AT, nor does the farmer's market match those of PT. This section deals with principles of appropriate design, first with the children's theatre and then with the market. The following section discusses the principles of PT in the same order.

AT projects are *long in labour and short in capital* (as suggested by Schumacher, 1973, p. 19). This is true of most design-build projects, since building with students who are new to design and construction is inherently labour intensive. Time is taken to teach students techniques, to consider the design implications of construction and to show how to be more efficient communicators with those building the project. However, a large investment in labour is a consequence of design/build rather than a principled position.

The children's theatre and the farmers' market were both labour intensive. The theatre required a huge number of students for a short period of time, and the market ranged from four to ten students over seven months. In both cases, the land was donated and grant funds paid for the construction materials. The materials themselves differed. In the earlier project, standard construction materials were used, availability permitting. The local lumber yard stocked a large amount of sixteen-foot one-by-three strapping material normally used as furring for walls on older houses. In the later project, material was brought in from the closest source, a sawmill four-hundred kilometers away.

In the children's theatre, two factors combined to establish a technological palette: an incredibly tight timeframe of two weeks for design and construction and a conceptual interest in working with local ways of making. Localness is the distinguishing technical and social attitude of the project. In fact, the conceit of the project was to discover or develop a building culture (all in two weeks) suitable for the local Acadian people, who continue to fight English cultural assimilation. The project implies the possibility of a new, locally-focused way of building. For example, the rock-ballasted wooden cribwork of the theatre' walls was similar to the townspeople's way of building wharves. Our thin, bent-wood construction was similar to the light-weight cradles used to support landed boats during winter. However, suspending weighted walls did not make sense to locals steeped in North American building convention. On opening day, we had to quickly remove the backfill a local builder had retrofitted to 'correct' our construction. Our attempt to reveal the potential of two local building practices was concealed by our translation; the techniques were no longer seen as similar.

Our strategy of avoiding wind resistance needed to be constantly validated with discussion and reference to local stories. For example, townspeople believed that, during suettes, if a window or a door on the windward side of a building breaks, then one has to quickly open windows on the leeward side. Learning from this, we let some wind blow through both our projects. Often, locals expressed amazement at how our structures endured wind storms. This strategy reveals itself straightforwardly in the children's theatre, as is all about slatted walls. Technological transfer has been evident in recent billboards that now use slatted wall-like construction to let the wind through. The market, as opposed to the theatre, was all about a roof, and an unconventional one at that. As a prototype, however, it demonstrates a particular technique of light-weight building structure suitable for rural areas using simple tools and a low degree of capital investment.

According to Nieusma (2004), AT[10] is characterised by "(…) low investment cost per work-place, low capital investment per unit of output, organizational simplicity, high adaptability to a particular social or cultural environment, sparing use of natural resources, low cost of the final product or high potential for employment". Often, design/build projects are done on a 'shoe-string' budget for clients with little or no capital. In our case, in the intervening ten years we had developed the capacity to bring significant resources to the market project. This effectively increased the investment cost per work-place. If the children's theatre was priced low then the market was priced at a medium level. Both projects were low in capital investment, using simple tools and materials. The theatre design was based on organizational simplicity, with all connections, for example, being made with common deck screws with a simple set of rules for assembly (e.g. all 1x3s were lengthened past 16 feet with a one-foot lap to the outside fastened with three

---

[10] OECD. "Appropriate Technology". Glossary of Statistical Terms. [Retrieved 24 April 2011].

screws, the lap never happened at a vertical rib). The farmer's market was organized based on sophisticated modeling and structural calculation.

Nieusma (2004) has suggested " (...) the transferability of technology among contexts is far from straight forward. ... Technology scholars came to realize that differences between a technology's developmental context and its use context were significant". Quoting Willoughby (1990), he points to the lack of historical success for AT:

> "Developing AT required accounting for the needs of others by paying careful attention to the use context of that technology, as well as to local perspectives on the problem to be solved. Attention to contextual particularities became one of the guiding approaches to AT and, hence, unlike technology transfer scholars, AT thinking took design as the point of intervention".

The application of bentwood principles to 'contextual particularities' in the theatre is strong. Even in the farmer's market, the structural forces and shell integrity were heavily influenced by local wind conditions. Nieusma and Willoughby could be right; development and use are quite distinct since, by nature, technology is mobile. On the other hand, architecture is immobile, so use and development overlap. Buildings have to be constructed of AT, at least to some degree.

Nieusma (2004) explains AT as a precursor to alternative design movements such as universal design, participatory design, feminist design and ecological design. In terms of ecological design, the extreme wind is a reminder of the impossibility of resisting and dominating nature. In each project, the idea of becoming transparent to the wind allowed us to economise on materials and strength. Robustness was created by resilience. Creating a form that deflected the wind around it and letting the wind find a way through lessened the natural forces that the structure had to resist. Materials were reduced by reusing a surrealistic derelict playground as the immediate surroundings of the theatre. This created difficulties and opportunities. Rather than creating a blank site plan, we incorporated the slide into the design and located the theatre around it. This configuration doubled as an entrance both alternate and exciting.

Today, it is problematic that the OECD website redirects from the *Glossary of Statistical Terms* entry on AT to "environmentally sound technologies"[11]. This is symptomatic of thinking that allows wider application of different technologies. No

---

[11] Appropriate technology. Retrieved September 20, 2018, from https://en.wikipedia.org/wiki/Appropriate_technology. *Referencing OECD.* "Appropriate Technology". *Glossary of Statistical Terms.* Retrieved 24 April 2011

longer are they necessarily local, socially just, or acceptable to the building occupant. It changes the meaning of the term considerably and erases any distinction between the technologies of our two projects. In addition, the current OECD definition removes social issues from any technological project. Thus, universal design, participation and feminist design have been marginalized, as well as the understanding that all technologies are socially constructed. This essay continues using the earlier sense of AT that includes its social aspects.

SCALE OF INFLUENCE, SOME SOCIAL ASPECTS OF DESIGNING AND BUILDING

In conventional architectural studio projects, students work on their own ideas but are marginalised in the sense that they have no impact outside their instructor and closed circle of classmates. In design/build, however, designing, constructing, and meeting with real client groups expands this circle to include 'outsiders.' Group dynamics aside, students realise that their developing designs have to be evaluated by experiment and experience in order to perform in the real world. Students become designer-builders, sorting out details and working on sub-projects nested within the developing design framework. As a student, participation means coming to group decisions about design proposals as well as working with client groups and the local public. Potential for local adoption of design solutions, including new ways of construction, is essential to these projects.

Socially responsible design refers to a designer's ability to work in ways that confront dominant design outcomes and empower marginalized social groups (Nieusma, 2004). Children are an under-represented group. Thus, the theatre design was made for them in several ways, complementing the building program. The closest three tiers of bench seats and the risers between them were scaled to body size of three different ages of children, serving to attract them. Adults accompanying children had to negotiate an entry that varied from two-year-old height to twelve-year-old height, a wide, short opening that only children could pass under without stooping. A spiral slide created an alternative playful entry, again a product of considering children over adults.

Nieusma (2004) continues advocating the inclusion of those normally marginalised in his discussion of participatory design, emphasising that it is not just user-centred design. In both cases, the building program was established by and drew strength from the Chéticamp community: in one case, an Acadian-speaking theatrical troop with child actors depicting local histories and music and, in the other case, a market for local crafts and small businesses. The projects benefitted from a community that was fighting its marginalisation through effective programming, informing their critical view when presented with design options in public workshops.

Implicit in the processes of design-build is the architectural student walking in the shoes of the other. An often-forgotten user of architecture is the construction worker. Here, however, the student actively participates in the building processes they establish through design and detailing. The building of the children's theatre lacked the resources of conventional construction companies but made up for this by reacting to local conditions as opportunities. For instance, the rain that filled the excavation became a way of leveling it. Also, when its curved form would not accept easy scaffolding, the building created its own.

In the past, simple things like driving nails privileged men. Schools of architecture are now gender-balanced, though, and design/build programs take this into account. The contemporary construction site has leveled the gender gap through the use of power drivers and the predominance of screws for connecting wood. In general, tools help, but even more important is the construction process. In our case, the lightweight wood construction of the children's theatre created an accessible building process. Similarly, the grid shell used wood with a very small cross section, inherently and intentionally lightweight and easy to handle.

In their classic study on the origins of bicycle design, Bijker et al. (1984) discussed the influence of social groups on new technologies. Often, these groups are incohesive and hard to define. Nevertheless, the study argues that women had a huge influence that eventually led to widespread agreement on the best design. In our case, design-build extends these potential influences from design into the manner of construction. Inclusiveness is an attribute of simple materials and simple joinery.

PROTOTYPING

In the first half of the 20th century, the concept of the prototype was thought of as a physical model and as a conceptual strategy. It became important to the avant-garde and quickly traversed the artistic landscape of Europe (Küchler, 2010). This continues in a modified form today.

> "I find in Gell an amazing theoretical model for the subtle push and pull that operates within the relational networks surrounding the work of art—itself a locus for the complex interactions between (in Gell's terms) the artist, the work's recipients, and the prototypes it 'represents'" (Brookhenkel, 2009)[12].

An important feature of PT is the incorporation of failure as a legitimate and very often empirical part of the process. David Pye (1968) makes a distinction between a work of craft and a work of assembly predicated on- the issue of

---

[12] Referencing Gell (1998)

predetermination. For him, craft is a work of risk that "(...) depends on judgment, dexterity and care which the maker exercises as he works" (Pye, 1968, p.20). From the client's point of view, both projects were a work of risk. As we always made clear, the work of the students was subject to failure. It is possible that the final built work itself, while attempting to be permanent, would be incomplete or inhabitable and might have to be torn down. Of course, in this case, any arguments about AT would be moot.

Based on Pye (1968), the farmer's market was a work of certainty where the judgment, dexterity, and care were exercised during the design phase of the project. The project was designed and tested in the form of computer models and mock-ups. Important to note at this stage is that tests can fail and, in fact, should fail in order to establish reasonable limits. So, while there is risk, models and mock-ups mitigate the risk. Many things are predetermined. Nevertheless, since the project incorporates innovative techniques, there were pauses in the construction. It was not easy for the designers to fully visualise the work in three-dimensions because it was not orthogonal. These encounters with the unexpected happen more frequently than in more conventional construction. PT is definitely more prone to failures than works of certainty.

The following sequence from Le Marché Fermier illustrates the difficulty PT has with predetermination. The moment after the grid shell was erected, but before the project was completed, there was a straight forward conflict between multiple models. This occurred at the handing over of the project from the original student team to a second group. Each lath was marked with the location of each lath that it crossed. The group's task was to infill between the laths with shear blocks and in the process lock the nodes down into their final predetermined locations (this is seen by comparing the physical and digital models illustrated on Figures 6.8 and 6.9).

Though this was to be 'fine tuning' the structure, many of the laths would not comply. The obstinate wood laths refused to hit their marks, or more properly, when forced to hit their marks, they complained in various ways. Sometimes they broke, but more frequently they caused the overall form of the entire structure to change somewhere else in unexpected ways. We developed an eye for the form and realized that there was something off about the structure as it stood. The wood had a mind (or model) of its own and, after a couple of weeks of frustration, we decided to listen to it. We measured the built structure using a sophisticated piece of survey equipment that targeted each node and created a three-dimensional array to be exported as a computer model. There were now four versions of the building: the actual building, the architectural digital model, the structural digital model and the surveyed digital model. When we overlaid the three computer models, there were a number of discrepancies. It turned out that there had been a glitch in the architectural computer model that caused the misalignment when installing the laths (illustrated using the different overlaid model colors in Figure 6.9). It was an error that was found using the digital survey equipment and overlaid computer models.

After discovering the discrepancy in the models, we could have left things as they were and added reinforcement to the structure to suit its new configuration. Instead, we rebuilt it over the next few months into a form between its original architectural and structural models. The wood happily glided into its new locations and the shear blocking was completed before the onset of winter. The act of rebuilding was true to the principle of PT. Nothing would be gained in the overarching project that was 'grid shell development' if we responded to the mistake instead of erasing it as extraneous to the experiment.

Another issue that differentiates AT and PT is physical failure. Local construction strategies have proven successful in terms of building performance in local conditions, adapting local techniques such as cribwork to building needs. The designer and the builder are responsible for the translation and the correct adaptation of building principles. For example, the curvature in the theatre plan was based on the maximum bending that one-by-threes would tolerate. This was tested on-site by moving several pieces of wood into a curve and gauging the point of breakage. Luckily, the wood was still fairly green and, able to adapt to its curvature and make future breakage less and less probable. Physical failure of a prototype is far more generalizable. It is attempting to extend the application of a particular technique. Failure or success in this case builds on advances from recent allied research. In our case, we adapt existing technology to suit extreme climates and push it to be thinner and lighter. In addition, since it will be an active building, the social aspects of the prototype can be considered such as ease of knowledge transfer and its suitability for various building programs.

The social aspects of technology need some elaboration. Two theoretical positions, the social construction of technology and actor-network theory, argue in different ways that technology is necessarily social. Innovation is either the product of sociality or an actor in a network that includes people and things. This view considers the inclusion of marginalized groups as part of socially responsible design.

As suggested earlier, effective knowledge mobilization is one indicator of success that both AT and PT share. Essentially, this is the question of whether a piece of technology is repeatable. Does the technique lend itself to easy replication or has sufficient knowledge been learned by others? Even if the technique has been translated successfully, too, a critical question remains. Are the projects scalable?

The exercise of comparing and contrasting these two projects and positions extends to a discussion of consequences. Appropriate technology takes into account local implications through reinterpretation. However, it became clear that this reinterpretation was not evident and needed to be explained. There exists some evidence that letting wind pass through structures has been recognized as a legitimate building strategy, but the reapplication has been restricted to things like roadside signs. Appropriate technology it seems is subject to a few consequences: it recedes into the local context and its transitions of form are more evident that its transitions of process. In effect, it is not easily scalable.

PT and experimentation are prevalent modes of knowledge production. PT intends global and local implications through knowledge mobilization. Here the impact is scalable and wide-ranging. Nevertheless, despite its use of simple construction technologies its sophisticated design technologies inspire wonder rather than comprehension. The search is still for a truly locally-accessible, contemporary, sustainable building practice.

Recently, the projects undertaken by Coastal Studio are being recorded and analyzed by sociologists. This reflects an interesting development in knowledge creation. There has been a shift in emphasis from the experimental as a knowledge-site to the experimental as a social process (Jiménez, 2014). The experimental and open-ended qualities of PT have become a surrogate for new cultural experiences and processes of democratisation. PT is something that "happens to social relationships when one approaches the craft and agency of objects in particular ways" (Jiménez, 2014). Where researchers once entered the field as outsiders (academics), they are now suddenly and unexpectedly being turned into insiders (colleagues, advisors). The traditional entry and exit points of knowledge-creation now face a permanent threat of abduction and destabilization (Mosse, 2006).

Coastal Studio is developing a rigorous way of working in design/build. Here the use of the terminology of PT is apt. Collaboration with other university design/build programs has made a comparative analysis of methodology possible. Projects are aligned in a series, each project learns from previous ones. Knowledge transfer is recorded. The collaboration on a sequence of prototypes parallels current tendencies where software designers release beta or work-in-progress versions of their programmes as an invitation for others to contribute their own developments and closures.

CONCLUSION

This comparison between the market and the theatre has been an opportunity to reflect on the possibility of a theoretical basis for design/build in technology and design studies. Here, Coastal Studio is beginning work that has all the dimensions of architectural research — practice, method, and theory — where the study of technological innovation and the social and experiential aspects of the space are the focus of scholarship about architecture.

As Cedric Price famously quipped in 1966 "*Technology is the answer, but what was the question?* [emphasis added]" And, how does architecture operate in a pluralist world where there are no clear questions. Is architecture reactionary? Perhaps. However, if it reacts, then the problems must be multiple and not singular. We have seen where the modernist singularity led us, even as it espoused socially progressive ideals. In a world of multiple technologies, in what ways can architecture operate for the public good (as our code obliges us to do), and should we be reconsidering our professional ethics? Clarity around the strategies for building technology is an important part of the mix. The contextual nature of AT and the global nature of the PT agenda need to be clarified and challenged.

REFERENCES

Adriaenssens, S., Block, P., Veenendaal, D., & Williams, C. (2014). *Shell structures for architecture : form finding and optimization.* Routledge.

Bijker, W. E., Hughes, T. P., Pinch, T., & Pinch, T. J. (1984). *The social construction of technological systems : new directions in the sociology and history of technology.* MIT Press.

Binder, T., Brandt, E., Ehn, P., & Halse, J. (2015). Democratic design experiments: between parliament and laboratory. *CoDesign, 11*(3–4), 152–165. https://doi.org/10.1080/15710882.2015.1081248

Brookhenkel. (2009, February 11). Week 4: The Art Nexus. *Thing Theory.* https://thingtheory2009.wordpress.com/2009/02/10/week-4-the-art-nexus/

Blundell-Jones, P. (2002). *Modern architecture through case studies.* Architectural Press.

Callon, M., Lascoumes, P., & Barthe, Y. (2009). Acting in an uncertain world : an essay on technical democracy. MIT Press.

Cavanagh, T. (2013). Innovative Structures and the Design-Build Model of Teaching. In A. Zarzycki & R. Dermody (Eds.), *Proceedings of the 2013 Building Technology Educators' Society Conference* (pp. 405–410).

Cavanagh, T., Kroeker, R., & Mullin, R. (2005). For Want of Wind. *Journal of Architectural Education, 58*(4), 6–11. https://doi.org/10.1162/1046488054026741

Chilton, J., & Tang, G. (2017). *Timber gridshells architecture, structure and craft.* Routledge.

Foster, H. (1987). Concluding Notes. In R. McCarter (Ed.), *Building, Machines* (p. 63). Princeton Architectural Press.

Gell, A. (1998). Art and Agency: Towards an Anthropological Theory. Clarendon Press.

Guggenheim, M. (2014). From Prototyping to Allotyping. *Journal of Cultural Economy, 7*(4), 411–433. https://doi.org/10.1080/17530350.2013.858060

Guy, S., & Farmer, G. (2001). Reinterpreting Sustainable Architecture: The Place of Technology. *Journal of Architectural Education, 54*(3), 140–148. https://doi.org/10.1162/10464880152632451

Hill, J. (2010). Prototypes and primitive huts. *Visual Communication, 9*(3), 323–340. https://doi.org/10.1177/1470357210372720

Jasanoff, S. (2012). Acting in an Uncertain World: An Essay on Technical Democracy (review). *Technology and Culture, 53*(1), 204–206. https://doi.org/10.1353/tech.2012.0016

Jiménez, A. C. (2014). Introduction - The prototype: more than many and less than one. *Journal of Cultural Economy, 7*(4), 381–398. https://doi.org/10.1080/17530350.2013.858059

Jorgensen, E. (2005). Four Philosophical Models of the Relation between Theory and Practice. *Philosophy of Music Education Review, 13*(1), 21-36.

Küchler, S. (2010). The prototype in 20th-century art. *Visual Communication, 9*(3), 301–312. https://doi.org/10.1177/1470357210372723

MacKay-Lyons, B., & Buchanan, P. (2008). *Ghost: building an architectural vision.* Princeton Architectural Press.

Macy, C. (2008). *Free lab: Design-build projects from the School of Architecture, Dalhousie University, Canada, 1991-2006.* Tuns Press.

Mosse, D. (2006). Anti-social anthropology? Objectivity, objection, and the ethnography of public policy and professional communities. *Journal of the Royal Anthropological Institute, 12*(4), 935–956. https://doi.org/10.1111/j.1467-9655.2006.00371.x

Nieusma, D. (2004). Alternative Design Scholarship: Working Toward Appropriate Design. *Design Issues, 20*(3), 13–24. https://doi.org/10.1162/0747936041423280

OECD. "Appropriate Technology". Glossary of Statistical Terms. [Retrieved 24 April 2011].

Pye, D. (1968). *The nature and art of workmanship.* Studio Vista.

Schumacher, E. F. (1973). *Small is beautiful: a study of economics as if people mattered.* Blond & Briggs.

Verderber, S., Cavanagh, T. & Oak, A. (2019). *Thinking While Doing: Explorations in Educational Design/Build.* Birkhauser.

Were, G. (2010). Special issue: prototypes. *Visual Communication, 9*(3), 267–272. https://doi.org/10.1177/1470357210372715

Willoughby, K. W. (1990). *Technology choice: a critique of the appropriate technology movement.* Westview Press.

EPILOGUE

Carmela Cucuzzella
Concordia University

Sherif Goubran
The American University in Cairo

This book took us on a journey that distances itself from the mainstream approaches for sustainable architecture. Our book stepped back to consider metrics, standards, and optimization methods in the broader context of the discipline and practice of architecture. The collection is not advocating for the elimination of such metrics or standards. Metrics and standards are key to guiding decisions. These are imperative and will continue to be as we move forward in seeking specific goals. But if they are adopted as the sole means to direct the design, then this results in architecture that is used as a means to reach environmental goals alone and not about designing places for living, working, playing, and contemplating. When the architecture only seeks to comply with the measurements expected and the enhanced optimizations, would this not produce simply a piece of equipment and not a space that is conceived for people?

Unsurprisingly, environmental architecture has been highly critiqued with respect to its integrity to the discipline, since, more often than is desired, it embraces the technical conditions, while leaving its formal qualities largely to chance. This collection is calling for the return of 'architecture' in sustainable architecture – and one that is equally focused on the appropriateness of the design for place and program, as well as metrics. With this collection, we aimed to open up the conversation about sustainable architecture to more carefully nuance how the measurements are directly related to the meaning, with repercussions in both theory and practice. We are calling for the repositioning of sustainable architecture so that designers can more willingly embrace these challenges in ways that are conducive to their own practice. We are not discrediting metrics but rather looking for ways forward – ways to complement them. The contributors for this collection searched, investigated and illustrated the different facets that make up this road ahead. From practitioners to educators, they showed us that there are many ways – beyond just the technical – to look at sustainable architecture: its making, elements and parameters.

Cormier shows that the digitalization of architecture has changed our perception and understanding of what is measurable. And that in our quest for sustainability, we have crossed all the architectural scales – from the molecular to the global. However, and beyond improvements in productivity, wellbeing or survival, we are still unsure how the diverse measurable elements of sustainability can lead us to build true architecture that is a source of timeless emotion and socio-cultural contribution.

Cucuzzella illustrates that sustainable architecture can have different – if not competing – ontologies. We often presume – both as designers and users – that a sustainable building is about its facticity; focusing on its measurable facts, and used to reduce impact, increase business potential and create more and hopefully *greener* economic growth. While this view of a building is limited, it is also severely constraining our ability to perceive the different ways a building can exist. Here, we specifically learn that sustainable architecture can also be for itself and for others. For itself, it refers to an architecture that can be a means for community development, urban regeneration, or even cultural impetus. For others, it refers to an architecture that is an exemplar for conservation, or a means for social cohesion and equity. By considering these broader ontological possibilities, we start to realize that a sustainable building can and should do much more than just reduce its impact and generate profits.

Tarkhan highlights that the market-driven practice and application of sustainable architecture has a strong and cyclical relation with technology. Demand pull, technology push and formalization are continuously reshaping the discourse of sustainable architecture and redefining the field in its entirety. However, this leaves us exposed to multiple risks – including over-reliance on specific proprietary technologies, governance of data and information issues, or shifting the field of sustainable design into a science of compliance. Tarkhan highlights that "while some areas of building sustainability have been impacted by technological advancements, it is important to reiterate that the degree of technological adoption should not be tantamount to defining the field".

While many of the contributions have highlighted the need to focus on the qualitative dimension of sustainable architecture, Tom Jefferies and Laura Coucill have placed their focus on metrics and sustainability data. They have shown us that capturing and representing data is crucial for developing effective sustainable design. They propose to use *culturally responsive analysis* to visualize the social and spatial consequences of sustainable design solutions—to make designs that respond to a real and measurable reality. Their contribution shows us that data, depending on how its represented, is not always objective. In fact, it becomes clear that using new and more design-led representations, such as culturally responsive analysis, creates the opportunity for recognising competing agendas and enables

Epilogue 145

the users to make value judgements around the application of the sustainable design technologies and interventions.

In the last two chapters, we have seen how these theoretical critiques can be embodied in practice. Amaral highlights that the tension between the technical or technological and sensorial or artistic is at the core of the architectural discipline. Amaral's application of the theory of tectonics illustrates that the process of making can be used to negotiate this tension – and enable us to create culturally relevant expressions as a dimension of sustainable architecture. Amaral's conclusion reminds us that sustainability is not only about using less (material, energy, space…) – but it is also about what, how and why we use.

Ted Cavanagh ends our collection with a fresh outlook on the place of technology in sustainable design. Cavanagh proposes that that technology, which can oscillate between the tailored and replicable, is just one dimension in the complex matrix of sustainable projects. The chapter made it clear that both the contextual nature of appropriate technology and the global nature of the prototyping technology agendas need to be clarified and challenged – using practice, method and theory. In line with the established critique of technology, Cavanagh concludes the chapter and the collection by reminding us that technology rarely provides us with solutions. In the case of sustainable design, it appears that technology is continuously pushing towards more quantification and measurement. But as sustainable architecture is pulled more by the currents of measurements, what meanings are being lost?

As Brian Sinclair has so clearly described in the forward, modern civilization, in many cases, has fragmented our realities into discreet parts so that they can be counted and measured. And that if it cannot be counted, it doesn't count. In cases where these parts cannot be measured, we have resorted to dichotomies that cut up our vision of the world further. We can see how this cannot end well.

As we see in the contributions in this book, perhaps, a reflection on architecture founded on a dialogue with the circumstances within which humans live is not only relevant today. Could this be a way forward in theorizing the relevance of environmental architecture, not only for the benefit of the environment but for the discipline of architecture?

INDEX

A

aesthetics, 6, 29, 38, 97, 98, 100, 105, 114
air, 16, 18, 28, 49, 52, 53, 58, 61
appropriate technology, 117, 122, 123, 124, 133, 134, 135, 136, 138, 139, 141, 145
assessment, 3, 29, 50, 52, 62, 70, 73, 75, 78, 93, 99

B

behaviour, 3, 56, 81, 83, 84, 120
    human behaviour, 5, 49, 81, 92

C

certification, 3, 17, 47, 52, 53, 54, 64, 65
climate change, 2, 36, 39, 93, 98, 112
comfort, 16, 25, 50, 51, 53, 57, 60
complexity, 3, 4, 5, 50, 71, 73, 75, 78, 79, 91, 93
craft, 8, 97, 98, 105, 108, 109, 112, 114, 137, 140
critique, 24, 109, 145
cultural, 3, 6, 7, 23, 26, 30, 31, 71, 72, 73, 74, 76, 77, 78, 79, 81, 85, 87, 88, 89, 91, 92, 93, 105, 108, 109, 110, 114, 126, 134, 140, 144
    culturally responsive, 71, 72, 78, 144
    culturally responsive analysis, 72, 79, 87, 88, 91
culture, 31, 37, 42, 63, 72, 79, 91, 93, 98, 104, 124, 128, 134

D

data, 16, 63, 76, 83, 85
    data representation, 8, 83
design approaches, 2, 3, 5, 71, 72, 74
determinant, 46, 62, 102
digital, 15, 19, 21, 47, 55, 57, 61, 65, 77, 78, 79, 83, 84, 85, 86, 130, 131, 138
    digital communication, 21
    digital model, 4, 130, 131, 138
    digitalization, 4, 144
dimension, 6, 8, 14, 15, 19, 20, 21, 23, 26, 27, 45, 69, 72, 97, 100, 104, 105, 108, 114, 138, 140, 144, 145

E

eco-features, 5, 32, 36, 37, 39
eco-friendly, 24, 114
effective, 33, 55, 70, 71, 72, 77, 81, 91, 93, 136, 139, 144
    effectiveness, 8, 69, 70, 71, 72, 79, 93
efficiency, 2, 3, 8, 18, 20, 24, 26, 29, 33, 45, 49, 51, 52, 63, 65, 69, 70, 71, 72, 73, 74, 75, 77, 78, 79, 81, 83, 91, 93, 104, 108
    eco-efficiency, 2, 24, 26
emissions, 2, 3, 99
energy, 2, 3, 4, 14, 20, 26, 28, 29, 30, 32, 33, 37, 39, 49, 51, 52, 53,

63, 65, 72, 74, 75, 78, 79, 80, 81, 83, 89, 92, 93, 104, 145
energy infrastructure, 2, 79, 89
environment, 2, 4, 5, 14, 16, 21, 28, 29, 31, 36, 38, 42, 46, 49, 53, 55, 59, 61, 62, 63, 72, 73, 74, 75, 76, 77, 78, 85, 92, 98, 103, 134, 145
environmental, 1, 2, 3, 4, 5, 6, 7, 17, 21, 23, 24, 26, 28, 29, 32, 33, 36, 37, 38, 42, 49, 53, 56, 57, 60, 63, 70, 71, 72, 73, 74, 76, 78, 79, 81, 98, 108, 109, 114, 143, 145
  environmental accounting, 5, 72
  environmental degradation, 2, 7
  environmental hazards, 17
  environmental management, 3, 4, 5
  environmental parameters, 56, 60
  environmental preconditions, 71, 72
  environmental quality, 57, 63
  environmental technologies, 4, 30
  techno-environmental, 64
evaluation, 3, 5, 17, 26, 47, 55, 61, 65, 73, 75, 79
  re-evaluation, 70, 71, 83
experimentation, 106, 140

F

fresh air, 18, 36, 51, 54, 58

G

green, 3, 4, 7, 19, 25, 36, 37, 38, 40, 52, 53, 78, 99, 127, 139
grid, 2, 89, 117, 128, 130, 132, 133, 137, 138, 139

H

health, 17, 52, 53, 55, 58, 108
heating and cooling, 33, 74
human body, 15, 16, 17, 105

I

immaterial, 8, 97, 99, 101, 107, 108, 114
infrastructure, 2, 55, 56, 70, 75, 77, 79, 83, 88, 89
intention, 1, 15, 28, 47, 49, 57, 70, 73

L

LEED, 19, 29, 38, 52, 53, 56, 73
local, 4, 6, 8, 26, 30, 31, 39, 62, 70, 72, 77, 81, 83, 88, 89, 91, 108, 109, 110, 117, 118, 119, 123, 124, 126, 128, 133, 134, 135, 136, 137, 139, 140
localness, 123, 134

M

measurement, xx, 1, 4, 7, 23, 28, 51, 52, 56, 58, 59, 60, 61, 69, 75, 143, 145
metrics, 8, 28, 51, 52, 65, 69, 70, 73, 74, 75, 77, 78, 81, 84, 143, 144

N

nature, 3, 5, 16, 20, 25, 26, 39, 48, 50, 61, 63, 78, 79, 99, 100, 103, 107, 108, 114, 130, 135, 141, 145

O

occupant, 49, 50, 51, 52, 55, 56, 59, 61, 63, 136
ontology, 24, 25, 27, 40
optimize, 49, 111

P

paradigm, 6, 19, 21, 74, 85, 97, 103, 109
passive, 25, 26, 29, 48, 50, 76
perception, 7, 23, 26, 27, 28, 32, 33, 36, 37, 38, 39, 40, 42, 59, 61, 91, 98, 99, 104, 105, 107, 108, 144
performance, 2, 3, 5, 18, 24, 28, 29, 37, 49, 50, 51, 52, 53, 55, 60, 61, 62, 70, 71, 72, 73, 74, 75, 77, 78, 80, 81, 83, 85, 87, 88, 91, 93, 127, 128, 139
    performance verification, 60
phenomenology, 25, 98, 104
    phenomenological ontology, 25
physiological effects, 52, 54
potential, 23, 24, 25, 26, 27, 30, 31, 32, 33, 34, 35, 40, 42, 49, 50, 55, 61, 80, 81, 83, 85, 92, 93, 97, 100, 101, 108, 113, 134, 136, 137, 144
    potentiality, 25, 29, 32, 35, 36, 40
productivity, 19, 53, 144
prototyping, 117, 118, 122, 123, 125, 145

Q

qualitative, 1, 6, 8, 45, 48, 69, 75, 144
quantitative, 1, 4, 6, 23, 57, 69

S

scale, 2, 4, 5, 14, 15, 17, 18, 19, 20, 21, 25, 26, 29, 35, 46, 49, 50, 55, 57, 65, 73, 74, 76, 77, 78, 80, 81, 89, 99, 109, 113, 117, 123, 125, 128
    immaterial scales, 99, 101
    scalar, 4, 46, 47, 48, 55, 61, 62, 65, 70, 71, 79
    scales of sustainability, 14, 20, 21
site, 7, 29, 30, 31, 33, 35, 39, 74, 105, 106, 108, 110, 111, 120, 126, 127, 135, 137, 139
smart, 25, 26, 51, 77, 78, 85, 92, 93
    smart cities, 78, 83
social, 3, 4, 6, 7, 23, 24, 48, 64, 70, 71, 72, 74, 75, 76, 78, 79, 81, 85, 105, 114, 118, 125, 134, 136, 137, 139, 140, 141, 144
society, 2, 4, 6, 21, 28, 30, 42, 70, 76, 78, 79, 89, 93, 109
    societal benefit, 72
standard, 15, 16, 55, 59, 119, 123, 133
standardization, 123
sun, 18, 39, 49, 59
    sunlight, 18
sustainability, 1, 3, 4, 5, 6, 7, 14, 18, 19, 20, 21, 23, 24, 26, 27, 28, 30, 32, 34, 36, 38, 39, 42, 47, 48, 49, 51, 52, 62, 64, 65, 69, 70, 71, 72, 73, 74, 75, 77, 78, 79, 80, 81, 88, 91, 92, 98, 99, 104, 108, 109, 118, 144, 145
    smart sustainability, 78
    sustainability crisis, 1
    sustainability debate, 21
sustainable
    sustainable architecture, 1, 3, 4, 5, 6, 7, 8, 23, 24, 25, 26, 28, 29, 30, 31, 32, 33, 34, 35, 36,

37, 38, 39, 40, 42, 45, 69, 70, 72, 91, 97, 102, 117, 143, 144, 145
sustainable behaviour, 71, 72, 91
sustainable outcomes, 70, 72, 91
sustainable space, 70, 74, 75, 76, 79, 91
symbol, 37, 100, 111
  symbolic, 6, 25, 26, 100, 101, 102, 103, 105, 108, 111, 114
  symbolism, 31, 34, 36, 37

T

technical, 2, 7, 29, 45, 48, 76, 80, 87, 88, 89, 91, 97, 99, 100, 101, 103, 105, 114, 123, 134, 143, 145
technology, 2, 3, 6, 15, 26, 28, 29, 30, 31, 32, 33, 45, 48, 49, 50, 51, 53, 55, 60, 62, 63, 64, 65, 69, 75, 76, 77, 85, 86, 92, 108, 117, 118, 119, 122, 123, 124, 125, 135, 136, 139, 140, 141, 144, 145
  eco-technologies, 1, 5, 7, 28, 30, 33
  emerging technological frameworks, 51, 55

renewable technologies, 80
sensor technology, 46, 49, 50, 55, 63, 64, 65
tectonics, 8, 97, 98, 99, 100, 101, 104, 105, 106, 107, 108, 114, 145
theory, 7, 48, 63, 72, 89, 97, 98, 99, 100, 101, 103, 104, 108, 112, 114, 117, 118, 119, 133, 139, 140, 143, 145
transformation, 18, 19, 49, 105, 114
transportation, 2, 104
typology, 48, 49, 79, 89

V

Volatile Organic Compounds, 53, 54, 56

W

water, 2, 28, 29, 33, 51
WELL, 52, 56, 59, 60
wellness, 45, 47, 51, 52, 53, 55, 56, 62, 65
wood, 100, 101, 108, 109, 112, 114, 119, 120, 125, 126, 130, 134, 137, 138, 139

www.ingramcontent.com/pod-product-compliance
Lightning Source LLC
Chambersburg PA
CBHW050639300426
44112CB00012B/1866